CUTE FELT BEARS

CUTE FELT BEARS

20 EASY-TO-MAKE PROJECTS

Benjamin Rowling

BARRON'S

For Michael, the other friendly, creative bear in the forest

First edition for North America published in 2014 by Barron's Educational Series, Inc.

First published in the United Kingdom in 2014 by Fil Rouge Press Ltd
Conceived, edited and designed by Fil Rouge Press Ltd, 110 Seddon House, Barbican, London EC2Y 8BX

All inquiries should be addressed to :
Barrons's Educational Seres, Inc.
250 Wireless Boulevard, Hauppauge, New York 11788
www.barronseduc.com

ISBN: 978-1-4380-0504-1

Library of Congress Control No. 2013922425

FIL ROUGE PRESS
Publisher: Judith More
Editor: Jenny Latham
Designer: Janis Utton
Project photography: Lily More
Instructional photography: Michael Craven

9 8 7 6 5 4 3 2 1

Printed in China

contents

introduction

Bears! Big bears, little bears, majestic real bears, funny imaginary bears, scary bears, bears in art, bears in music, and bears in fashion. Basically I am obsessed with bears. And I guess you must be too if you have bought this book!

When I started making bears, I looked at crafting books and then put them down very fast. They were too difficult for a beginner. And when I became more experienced I picked up, and then put down, books even faster because they were too easy. So when I was writing this book, I wanted to create projects for everyone. Some are very simple to make, some may introduce you to new skills, some need patience and time to get right, but all of them have clear instructions and photographs to help you create successful pieces.

The "Bear Necessities" chapter provides information on all the tools and materials you'll need and also supplies some useful hints and tips on sewing techniques. This not a book full of complicated stitches or difficult techniques, but sometimes we all need a few simple instructions before we shout out, "Ah, that's how it's done!"

So have fun making the projects, and remember there is always, ALWAYS an opportunity to introduce more bears in to your life.

Benjamin

about TheBigForest

TheBigForest is a design company dedicated to bringing laughter, delight, and the handmade into your life. Want to find out about the creative folks in the forest hut? You have come to the right place.

After I'd finished school in costume and textiles, I really wasn't sure what I wanted to do next. The world of fashion didn't appeal, but I must design and create to be happy and I loved selling the goods I had made. TheBigForest started as a hobby, but soon Michael, our Head of Forestry Commissions, and I found lots of people who wanted to buy the goods we designed.

We are based in London, and also Brighton, England, on the sunny south coast in a cabin in the forest. The eagle-eyed among you will have spotted that

there aren't many cabins or indeed forests in either of those places, but we have managed to find huge and beautiful woods, a cabin with a view of the sea and dock in the summer and a warm wood burner and plenty of cake in the winter.

Our aim at TheBigForest is to design a constantly changing range of forest-themed goods, and although our brand is firmly rooted in British retro design, our inspiration comes from many different sources: mid-century textiles, the English illustrators Edward Bawden and Eric Ravilious, modernist Scandinavian design, Japanese cartoons, retro crafts from the 1950s to the 1980s, the buzz of a seaside city and, of course, the creative solitude of the forest.

TheBigForest is growing fast. Handmade animals for adults are only a small (but very important) part of what we do, and it's been so good to design greetings cards, paper-cut illustrations and prints, felt accessories and homewares, and to design and make large (and small) commissions and see them appreciated around the world.

Check out our blog (thebigforestuk.wordpress.com) to find out where to buy goods from TheBigForest, whether you want to make your purchase online or in a store. You can read all about our design adventures, commissions, and new goods there too. And our vision? To see all the wondrous goods designed by TheBigForest in every house and store across the world!

REALLY BEARY

Ok, let's face it; real bears are not the kind you invite around for tea! Bears are beautiful, majestic, wild creatures and deserve our respect. When I first became interested in bears, I saw lots of movies of bears in the wild and I encourage you to do the same because these animals are endlessly fascinating. The projects in this chapter take their inspiration from real bears, but they are not true likenesses. For example, the polar bear is too cuddly to be out in the snow, and I don't think that you'll find a Black Bear roaming around Yosemite park who looks exactly like the project on page 16, but he has kind of got the right snout and ears...well, I think so and I hope that you do too!

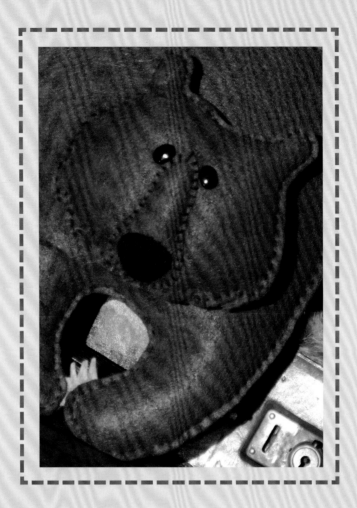

grizzly bear

*Time to get making with our first project. It's a crisp, graphic grizzly bear!
In real life these guys are best kept at a distance, but you can happily
hug our tame felt version.*

The carnivorous grizzly bear's formal name is *Ursus arctos horribilis,* and it's also known as the silvertip bear because of the gray or grizzled hairs in its brown fur. This bear is also called the North American brown bear as it lives in the uplands of western North America. You might be surprised to learn that all the national parks have regulations in place to protect grizzly bears because they are considered to be an endangered species in the U.S.A. and endangered in parts of Canada. So why not display this special grizzly bear figure in your home to raise awareness of the threat to its survival?

A

B

C

D

YOU WILL NEED

- Pattern templates (see pages 136-137)
- Basic sewing kit (see pages 123-125)
- 12 x 28 in. (30 x 70 cm) rusty brown felt
- Beige felt (scraps)
- Black felt (scraps)
- Black embroidery floss
- 2 x 10 mm black safety eyes
- Brown sewing thread
- Sewing machine
- Fiberfill (toy stuffing)

METHOD

1 Photocopy or trace the grizzly bear pattern pieces onto the pattern paper and cut out. You should have five paper pattern pieces: head, snout (a), snout (b), claws, body.

2 Pin the pattern pieces onto the felt. Use the rusty brown felt for the body, head, and snout (a), black felt for snout (b), and beige felt for the claws. Cut out. Repeat where two pieces are needed. You should have eight felt pieces: two body pieces, two head pieces and one snout in brown, one snout in black, and two claws in beige felt.

3 Sew the black snout piece to the brown snout piece using a running stitch and black embroidery floss. Position both snout pieces on the front head piece. Pin, then sew the snout to the head using black embroidery floss and straight stitch, and leaving a small gap for stuffing access, see **photograph A**.

4 Stuff the snout with fiberfill. Complete sewing to stitch the gap closed, securing the thread on the back of the work.

5 Position the eyes on the head. Make a small hole with scissors and push the safety eye post through the hole, see **photograph B**. Push the washer onto the post at the back of the head to secure.

6 Place the back piece of the head onto the front of the body and pin, see **photograph C**. Using a sewing machine and brown sewing thread, sew three or four lines of stitching in the center to secure, see **photograph D**.

7 Pin the front head piece on top of the back head piece and, with a 5 mm seam allowance, sew around the head using a running stitch and black embroidery floss, leaving a small gap for stuffing, see **photograph E**.

8 Stuff the head with fiberfill, see **photograph F**. Finish sewing the head together and knot the thread to finish.

9 Pin both claws to the back body of the bear, referring to the photograph of the finished bear on page 13 for positioning, and see **photograph G**.

10 Pin the front and back of the body wrong sides together and stitch together using running stitch and black embroidery floss, leaving a small gap for stuffing. Stuff the body with fiberfill, see **photograph H**.

11 Finish sewing the body together and knot the thread to finish.

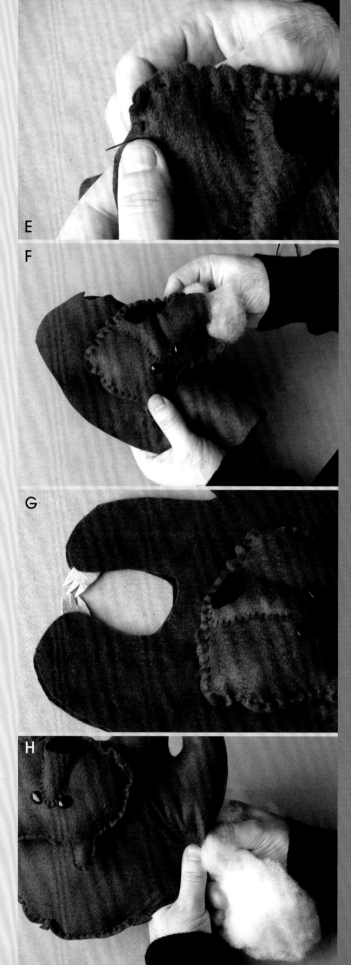

E

F

G

H

black bear
giant pillow

How about making a cushion with a bear's face? And here he is.
He makes people laugh and that can't be a bad thing, can it?

The black bear, or *Ursus americanus*, is a native of North America. Unlike its carnivorous cousin, the grizzly bear (see page 12), the majority of the black bear's diet consists of vegetation and insects such as bees and ants. However, they also love honey and will eat honeycombs despite the bee's stings. They mark trees with their teeth and claws as a way of communicating with other bears. The smallest North American bear at 5-6 ft. (1.5-1.8 m) high, this creature is not a true hibernator but spends winter months dormant in its den. One of the most common bears in North America, it's one of only two species worldwide not considered to be endangered. The original teddy toy was inspired by a story of President Roosevelt refusing to shoot a black bear cub, and the bear features in native American myths.

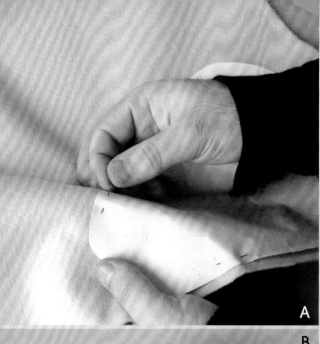

A

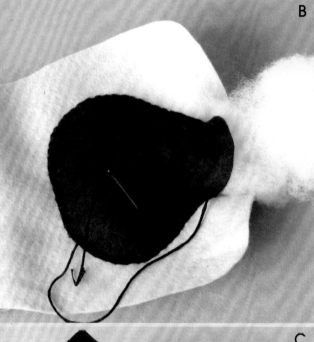

B

YOU WILL NEED

- Pattern templates (see pages 132-133)
- Basic sewing kit (see pages 123-125)
- 16 x 38 in. (40 x 95 cm) black felt
- 8 x 12 in. (20 x 30 cm) cream felt
- Black embroidery floss
- 2 x 15 mm safety eyes
- Fiberfill (toy stuffing)

METHOD

1 Photocopy or trace the black bear pattern pieces onto pattern paper and cut out. You should have three pieces: head, snout (a), snout (b).

2 Pin the pattern pieces onto the felt—use black for the head, cream for snout (a), and black for snout (b), see **photograph A**. Cut out. You should have four felt pieces: two head pieces and one snout in black, and one cream snout piece.

3 Pin the black snout (b) onto the cream snout (a). Sew in place using straight stitch and black embroidery floss, leaving a small gap for stuffing. Fill with fiberfill; you'll only need a small amount, see **photograph B**. Stitch the gap closed.

4 Using black embroidery floss and running stitch, sew the assembled snout onto the front of the head, see **photograph C**.

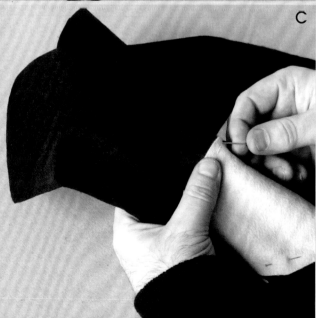

C

5 Position the safety eyes on the head, see **photograph D**. Make a small hole in the black felt with scissors and push the safety eye post through the hole. Push the washer onto the post at the back of the head to secure.

6 Pin the back of the head onto the front head piece. Leaving a 5 mm seam allowance, sew in place, using running stitch and black embroidery floss, leaving a small gap for the stuffing, see **photograph E**.

7 Stuff the black bear's head with fiberfill, see **photograph F**.

8 Finish sewing the head together, then knot the thread to finish.

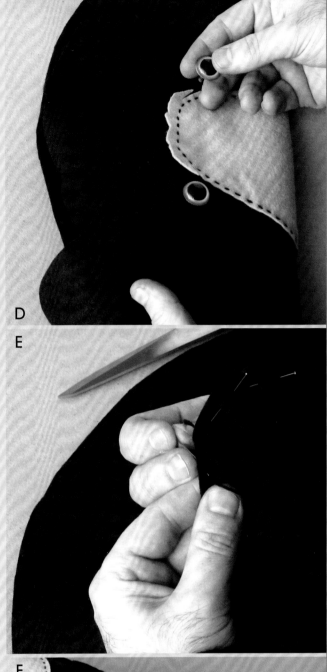

D

E

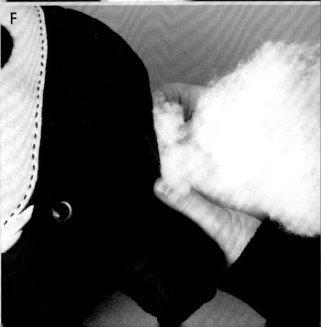

F

polar bear pillow

Bear silhouettes are endlessly fascinating, and here is a super-cool, wintry character that encourages you to stitch the iconic polar bear shape in white-out wool felt.

The polar bear, or *Ursus maritimus*, lives mostly within the Arctic Circle. As well as being the world's largest bear, it's also the world's largest land carnivore—its diet mostly consists of seals and it hunts them along the edge of the ice. A keen sense of smell helps this bear detect its prey over a mile away.

Polar bears are very good swimmers, which they do doggie paddle. Their paw pads are rough-surfaced, which helps them not to slip on the ice. The polar bear features in Inuit legends and myths, in particular the story of Nanook the polar bear god who could reward hunters with success or punish them.

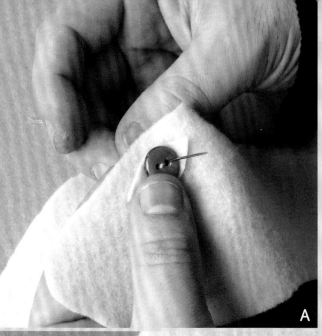

A

B

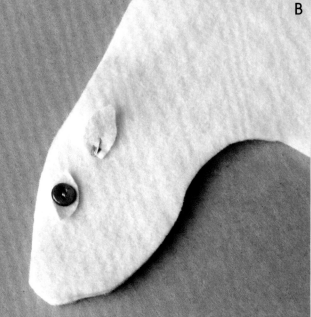

C

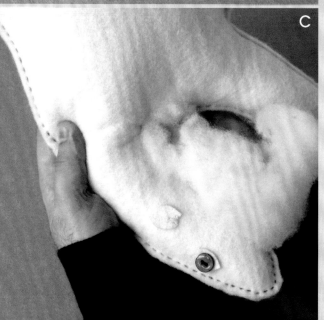

YOU WILL NEED

- Pattern templates (see pages 134-135)
- Basic sewing kit (see pages 123-125)
- 20 x 12 in. (50 x 30 cm) white 100 percent wool felt
- Off-white felt (scraps)
- Turquoise enamel coconut shell button, 13 mm
- Turquoise sewing thread
- Embroidery floss in pink and white
- Fiberfill (toy stuffing)

METHOD

1 Photocopy or trace the pattern pieces onto the pattern paper and cut out. You should have three pieces: body, ear, eye.

2 Pin the pattern pieces onto the felt. Use the soft 100 percent wool white felt to cut two pieces for the body and small scraps of the off-white for the ear and the oval shape behind the button eye. There's no ear or eye on the reverse of the polar bear.

3 Place the off-white felt oval shape behind the button that serves as an eye, then stitch the button and oval onto the head using turquoise sewing thread, see **photograph A**.

4 Stitch the ear onto the body using straight stitch and white embroidery floss, see **photograph B**.

5 Pin the back and front together, wrong sides facing. Leaving a 5mm seam allowance and using pink embroidery floss and running stitch, sew from the middle of the bear's back around the head and front paw to between the two paws. Stuff the front of the animal with fiberfill.

6 Continue to sew around the body, leaving a small gap for stuffing. Stuff the rest of the body using fiberfill, see **photograph C**. Finish sewing the body together and then knot the thread to finish.

The polar bear silhouette is loved for its elongated body, small
tail and ears, large, furry feet, and sharp claws.

sloth bear
bookmark

Sloth bears have a distinctive V or Y shape of lighter fur on their chest. I was going to make one for this project, but it made his body too thick to be a good bookmark. You can always add one if you want to, though.

The sloth bear, or *Melursus ursinus*, hails from the Indian subcontinent where, in the past, the bears were tamed and used as performing pets. They eat termites (and fruit) and with their long shaggy coat, a mane around the face, and the longest tail in the bear family they really are one of the most distinctive animals. Sloth bears have a slow, shambling walk but can also gallop quickly if they need to. But luckily your sloth bear bookmark isn't going anywhere—except in between the pages of your latest book, of course. Can't bear to lose your place? Well here is a silly sloth bookmark to help you keep track.

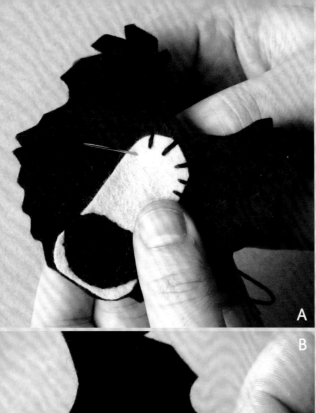

A

B

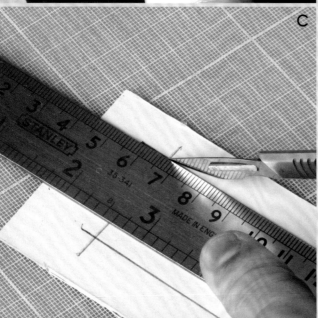

C

YOU WILL NEED

- Pattern templates (see pages 134 and 137)
- Basic sewing kit (see pages 123-125)
- 12 x 8 in. (30 x 20 cm) black felt
- Cream felt (scraps)
- Black embroidery floss
- Black sewing thread
- 2 x 5 mm black round plastic beads
- Thick cardstock
- Fiberfill (toy stuffing)

METHOD

1 Photocopy or trace the sloth bear pattern pieces onto the pattern paper and cut out. You should have five paper pattern pieces: head, snout (a), snout (b), bookmark, liner.

2 Pin the pattern pieces onto the felt. Use black for the sloth bear bookmark body, head, and snout (b), and cream for snout (a). Cut out. You should have four felt pieces: two bookmark pieces and one snout in black, and one snout in cream felt.

3 Stitch the black snout piece onto the cream snout piece using running stitch and black embroidery floss. Position the assembled snout on the head front, pin and sew in place using straight stitch and black embroidery floss, see **photograph A**.

4 Position the black bead eyes on the head front and sew in place using black sewing thread. Put to one side.

5 Setting it at a jaunty angle, sew the back head piece onto the front piece of the bookmark body using running stitch and black embroidery floss, see **photograph B**.

6 Cut the bookmark stiffening liner from thick cardstock, see **photograph C**.

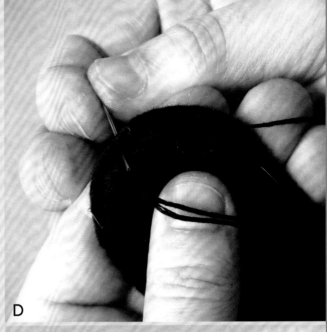

D

7 Pin both pieces of the bookmark body together with the cardstock in between.

8 Starting at the bottom, sew both pieces of the bookmark body together using running stitch and black embroidery floss, making sure that the cardstock liner stays in place, see **photograph D**. Ease the bear's head forward as you sew around it. Complete sewing at the bottom of the bookmark and knot the end to finish.

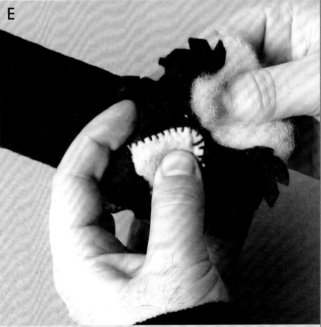

E

9 Pin the front and the back head pieces together, wrong sides together. Sew using a running stitch and black embroidery floss and leaving a small gap for stuffing the head, see **photograph E**. Stuff the head with fiberfill.

10 Finish sewing the head together and knot the thread to finish, see **photograph F**.

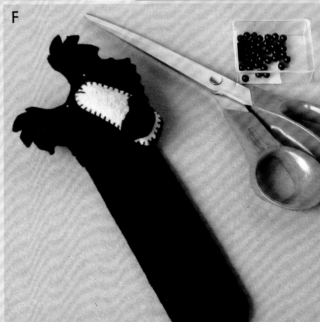

F

giant panda

Here is a pretty panda nibbling on a crunchy bamboo snack for you to make. It must be strange going through life looking so unbearably cute!

Referred to as the giant panda so it is not confused with the red panda, the black and white panda is formally known as *Ailuropoda melanoleuca*, which literally means "black and white cat-foot." In fact, its paws have the equivalent of five fingers and a thumb which help it hold the bamboo it eats. The panda's round face is due to big jaw muscles and teeth developed to break down the fibers of the bamboo which makes up 99 percent of their diet, although they also eat grasses. Pandas are native to China, and in the 1970s giant pandas were loaned by the People's Republic of China to overseas zoos. This practice has been called "Panda diplomacy."

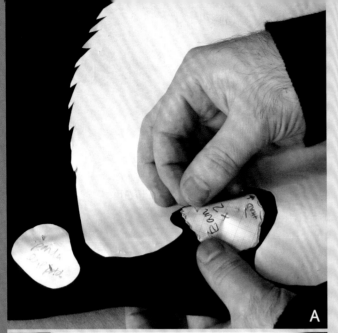

A

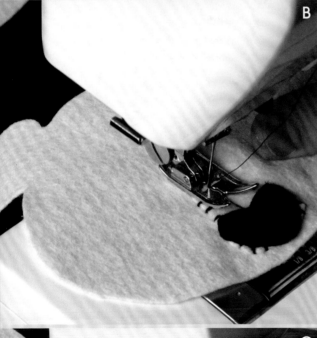

B

C

YOU WILL NEED

- Pattern templates (see pages 138-139)
- Basic sewing kit (see pages 123-125)
- 16 x 22 in. (40 x 55 cm) off-white felt
- 12 x 12 in. (30 x 30 cm) black felt
- 12 x 4 in. (30 x 10 cm) green felt
- Embroidery floss in black and green
- White and black sewing thread
- Sewing machine
- 2 x 5 mm black round plastic beads
- Fiberfill (toy stuffing)
- Wooden barbecue skewer
- Fine hacksaw

METHOD

1 Photocopy or trace the panda bear and bamboo pattern pieces onto the pattern paper and cut out. You should have nine pieces: body, body front, head, ear front, snout (a), snout (b), eye patch, bamboo branch, bamboo leaf.

2 Pin the pattern pieces onto the felt, see **photograph A**. We used black and off-white felt for the panda body, eye patches, ears, and snout, and green for the bamboo elements. Cut out. You should have 18 felt pieces: two white body and two white head pieces and one white snout, one black body front, two black eye patches, one black snout, two black ear pieces, and five green leaves and two green branches. Set to one side the bamboo pieces to make up later.

For Panda

1 Start by making the panda's head. Sew the black snout piece onto the white snout using running stitch and black embroidery floss.

2 Position the assembled snout on the head, pin, and then stitch in place using straight stitch and black floss.

3 Using white sewing thread (I used black here to show the position clearly) and a sewing machine, sew down the middle of the snout, see **photograph B**.

4 Position a black ear piece onto the left ear of the head piece and pin. Repeat with the right ear. Sew the left back and the front ear piece together, using a sewing machine and black sewing thread. Repeat with the right ear, see **photograph C**.

5 Sew a bead onto each eye patches using the photograph on page 29 as a guide. Position the eye patches on the head and sew all around using straight stitch and black embroidery floss, see **photograph D**. Put the head to one side.

6 Sew the black body front onto the white body front using a sewing machine and black sewing thread, see **photograph E**.

7 Place the back piece of the white felt head onto the front of the body and pin. Using a sewing machine and white sewing thread (we used black here to show the position more clearly), sew three or four lines of stitching, see **photograph F**, to secure.

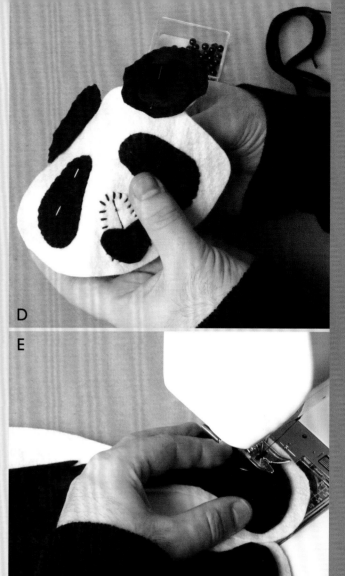

D

E

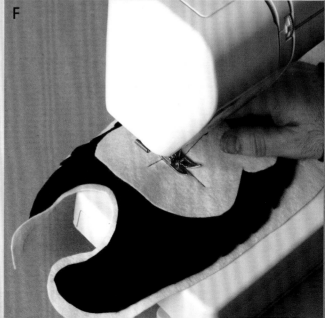

F

G

H

I

8 Pin the front and the back head pieces together, wrong sides together, and sew using a running stitch and the black embroidery floss, leaving a small gap for the stuffing, see **photograph G**.

9 Stuff the head with fiberfill, see **photograph H**. Finish sewing the head together and knot the thread to finish.

10 Pin the front and back of the body together, wrong sides together, and sew using running stitch and black embroidery floss.

11 Leave a small gap and stuff the body with fiberfill, see **photograph I**.

12 Finish sewing the body together and knot the thread to finish.

For Bamboo

1 Arrange the five leaves in a fan shape at the top of the bamboo branch, see **photograph** J. Using black embroidery floss, sew one end of the leaves onto the center of one end of the bamboo piece.

2 Cut a wooden barbecue skewer to slightly shorter than the bamboo felt piece, using a fine hacksaw.

3 Place the skewer on the wrong side of the felt piece, see **photograph K**. Fold the felt over the skewer and pin.

4 Sew along the bamboo stem to enclose the skewer, using green embroidery floss and a backstitch.

5 Trim the felt near the line of stitching, see **photograph L**.

Making Up

Sew the bamboo underneath the bear's snout with the black embroidery floss and a couple of straight stitches so that he looks as if he is eating the bamboo.

J

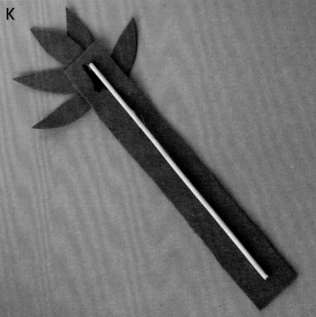

K

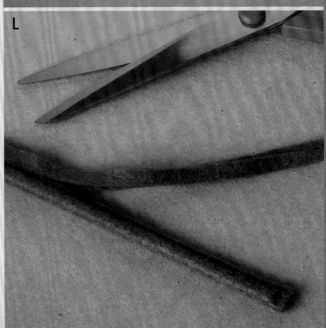

L

Left: The finished green bamboo branch is sewn just under the panda's nose.

PLUSH PRETENDERS

I love being told a story. It doesn't matter if it's a book or a movie; if the story is good then I'm hooked. Making up the story for each bear is where I start when I begin designing—who is he, what does he do in the forest, what is his character? In this chapter you will meet some interesting and unusual characters. Maybe they are a little quirky and a little, well, strange, but who wants to know (and to make) bears that follow the crowd? Inventing your bear's life story is great fun to do, and once you get started it's hard to stop adding more and more detail. Before you know it, you will have explained everything about the life of your bear and his days spent rambling around the forest.

making up
a bear's body

All the imaginary bears' bodies are the same, only the colors are different, so follow the instructions here, demonstrated on the Birthday Bear, for all the bears in this chapter, as well as the Autobearography Bear on page 72.

Start by making the body first, then go to the instructions for making the head front in your chosen project. Next, sew the head onto the front of the body, then come back to the body instructions on the following pages (38-41), and finally go back to the project to find out how to make the finishing details and accessories. Note that the matching stitching to the body is shown in black thread here so that the positioning is obvious, but you should match the sewing thread color you use to the body of your bear. However, the embroidery floss stitching should be in the recommended contrast color.

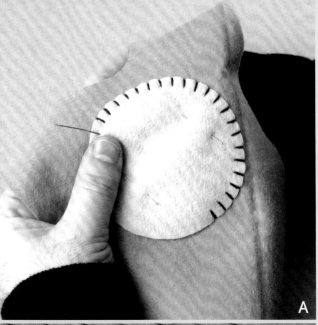

A

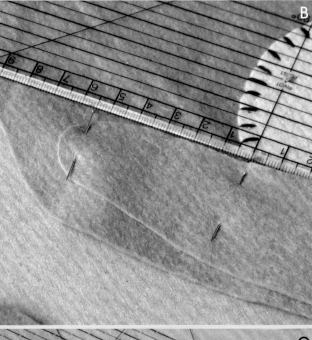

B

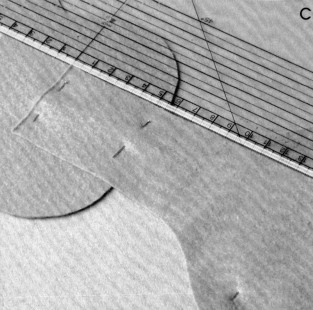

C

YOU WILL NEED

- Pattern templates (see pages 142-143)
- Basic sewing kit (see pages 123-125)
- Felt in the colors and amounts specified in your chosen project
- Sewing thread in a color to match your felt body
- Black embroidery floss
- Sewing machine
- Fiberfill (toy stuffing) and a wooden spoon

METHOD
Order of Work

1 Make the body stage one, following the instructions given below.

2 Go to the instructions for making the head front in the specific project.

3 Come back to the body instructions here, and sew the front of the head to the body (see Attaching the Head, stage two, on page 41).

4 Go back to the project instructions to make the finishing details and accessories.

Constructing the Body (Stage One)

● Trace body pieces onto pattern paper and cut out. You should have three pieces: body, paw, claw.

● Pin the paper pattern pieces onto the appropriate color felt. Cut out. You should have eight felt pieces: two body, four paw, and two claw pieces.

● Add any extra elements to the body front, such as the Birthday Clown Bear's tummy or the Santa's belt.

Birthday Clown Bear: Pin the tummy piece onto the body. Sew the tummy onto the bear using straight stitch and black embroidery floss, see **photograph A**. The other bears do not have a tummy piece.

Santa Bear: Cut the Santa belt from black felt. Cut the buckle from the yellow felt and using pinking shears cut around to create a jagged edge—see pattern templates, pages 144-145. Pin the buckle onto the belt and sew together using running stitch and black embroidery floss. Pin the belt across the bottom of the tummy and stitch in place using a sewing machine and black sewing thread.

● Position two paw pieces on the bear's body to form the paw backs. Pin at the top of the paw, then pin again 2¼ in. (5.5 cm) from the top of the paw, see **photograph B**. These pins are your guide for sewing the paws onto the body. Repeat with the other paw.

● Turn over the front body piece so that you are working on the wrong side. Take the back main head piece and pin to the body, with the bottom of the head around 2 in. (5 cm) from the top of the neck and with the body neck on top of the head piece, see **photograph C**.

● Using a color to match your bear's body (we only used black here to show the position clearly), machine two lines of stitching between the pins to secure the paw, see **photograph D**. Repeat with the second paw.

● Machine a square of stitching to secure the head to the neck, see **photograph E**. Leave a seam allowance of around 5 mm from the edge.

● Turn over the front body piece so that it's right side up.

● For the Valentine's Bear, see the instructions on page 55 for sewing on his tattoo.

● Position the front paw on top of the paw back you have already sewn onto the bear's body and pin, see **photograph F**. Repeat with the other paw.

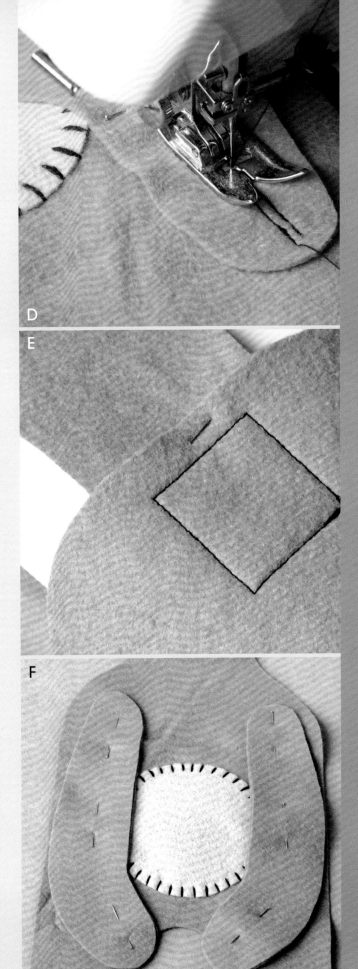

D

E

F

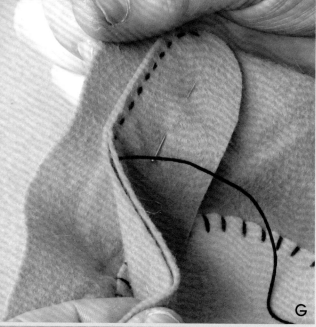

G

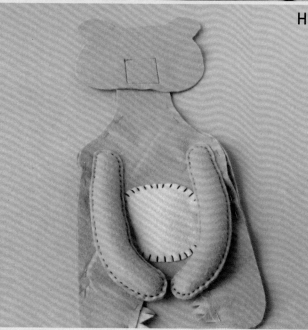

H

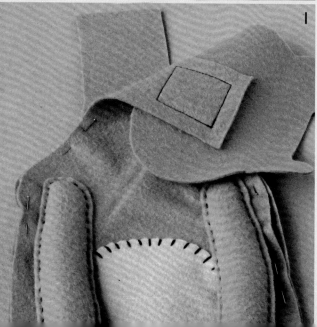

I

- Knot your embroidery floss and bring your needle up from behind the top of a paw. Using running stitch, start to sew the paw front, paw back, and the body together, see **photograph G**, attaching the top of the paw to the body.

- When you have sewn approximately 2½ in. (6 cm) from the top of the paw, stop sewing the paw to the body but continue sewing the paw back and front together, making sure that you don't sew the paw onto the body!

- Continue sewing until you have a small gap at the top of the paw for stuffing. Stuff with fiberfill.

- Finish sewing the paw to close the gap, bringing the floss to the back of the work to secure.

- Repeat with the second paw.

- Position the front body onto the back body, wrong sides together.

- Pin the claws between the two lower paw pieces that are integral to the body, see **photograph H**.

- Using thread to match the body felt color, machine stitch around the body 5 mm from the edge, being careful to move the head and the paws gently out of the way as you sew, see **photograph I**. Do not sew across the top of the neck!

- Turn the bear over and stuff the body through the neck, see **photograph J**. Push the fiberfill down into the body using the handle of a wooden spoon.

- Using black embroidery floss, sew the neck together using two lines of running stitch, see **photograph K**.

Working the Head

● Now go to the instructions for your chosen bear to find out how to make the head front.

● Once you have made the head front, come back to these instructions to complete your bear.

Attaching the Head (Stage Two)

● Place the front of the head onto the back of the head at the top of the body. Pin the ears to line up the front and back and then pin around the head.

Surfer Bear: Pin the fur between the front and the back of the head, using the photograph of the finished bear on page 56 as a guide to positioning.

● Leaving a 5 mm seam allowance, sew the front and the back of the head together using running stitch and black embroidery floss, see **photograph L**. Don't sew the front of the head onto the body at this stage—leave a small gap for stuffing.

● Stuff the head using fiberfill.

● Finish sewing the head to close the gap, bringing the floss to the back of the work to secure.

J

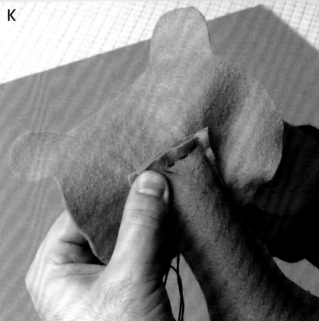

K

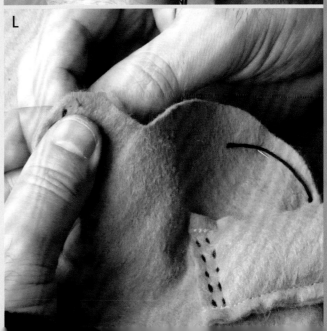

L

vampire bear

Of course he's not really a blood sucker, but he has a very cool costume which is a bit scary, although we all know he is very sweet. Actually, all he wants to do is sink his fangs into the trick-or-treat candy or maybe a cookie.

Do you think they are real fangs? I'm not convinced to be honest, but I don't want to get too close just in case. Like all good vampires, our Halloween Vampire Bear also has a long, flowing cape with a big collar to keep out the chilly October winds and, to make him complete, he also has a big mustache. I love bears with mustaches, and rosy cheeks too. It makes them look like they don't take themselves seriously and that's a good thing when you meet a bear for the first time. So say "Hi, Vampire Bear!" and don't tell him that his eyes look like they have seen a ghost.

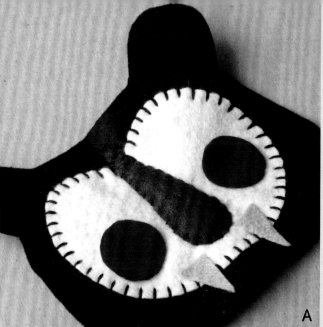

A

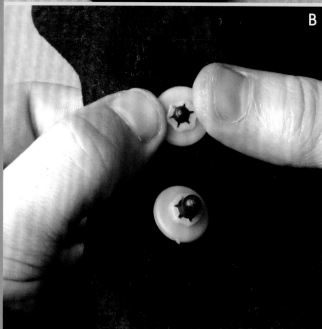

B

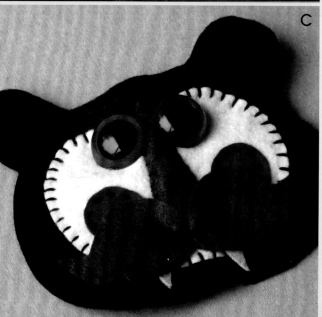

C

YOU WILL NEED

- Pattern templates (see pages 141, 142-143, 144)
- Basic sewing kit (see pages 123-125)
- 14 x 22 in. (35 x 55 cm) black felt for body, paws, head
- 2 x 6 in. (5 x 15 cm) brown felt for the mustache
- 8 x 12 in. (20 x 30 cm) red felt for cheeks, cloak, and claws
- Dark red felt for snout (scraps)
- 6 x 4 in. (15 x 10 cm) off-white felt for head front (b)
- Beige felt for fangs (scraps)
- Black embroidery floss
- Red, beige, and black sewing thread
- 2 x 20 mm red safety eyes
- 28 in. (70 cm) red velvet ribbon
- Sewing machine
- Fiberfill (toy stuffing)

METHOD

Make the body (stage one) first—see pages 38-40 for body instructions—in black felt. You should have eight pieces: two body and four paw pieces in black felt and two claw pieces in red felt. Then go to the instructions for making the head front, given here. Next, go back to the body instructions on page 41 and sew the front of the head to the body. Finally, return here for the instructions to make the cloak.

Head Front

1 Photocopy or trace the head pieces onto the pattern paper and cut out. You should have six paper pattern pieces: head, head front, cheeks, mustache, snout, fangs.

2 Pin the pattern pieces onto the felt. Cut out. You should have nine felt pieces: two black heads, one white head front, two red cheeks, two beige fangs, one brown mustache, one dark red snout.

3 Take the white head front piece and position it on top of the black head front. Pin. Sew in place using straight stitch and black embroidery floss.

4 Position the dark red snout on the head front and pin. Sew in place using straight stitch and black embroidery floss, leaving a small gap. Stuff with fiberfill. Stitch across the gap to close.

5 Position the cheeks and fangs, see **photograph A**. Pin, then sew the cheeks in place using running stitch and black embroidery floss.

6 Pin fangs in place. With beige sewing thread, sew a couple of stitches to secure them to the head.

7 Position the eyes on the head. Make a small hole with scissors and push the safety eye post through the hole, see **photograph B**. Push the washer onto post at the back of the head to secure.

8 Position the mustache and, using black embroidery floss, sew in a star shape to secure, see **photograph C**.

Cloak

1 Photocopy or trace the cloak pattern piece onto the pattern paper and cut out.

2 Pin the pattern pieces onto the felt. Cut out. You should have two red cloak pieces. Cut two pieces of velvet ribbon, each 14 in. (35 cm) long. Position one length of the ribbon on either side of the back cloak piece and pin (see pattern for the ribbon position). Pin the top and the bottom of the cloak together, see **photograph D**.

3 Machine sew the cloak together using red sewing thread, see **photograph E**, trapping the ribbon between the two layers.

4 Tie the two lengths of velvet ribbon in a bow to secure the cloak around the vampire bear's neck, see **photograph F**.

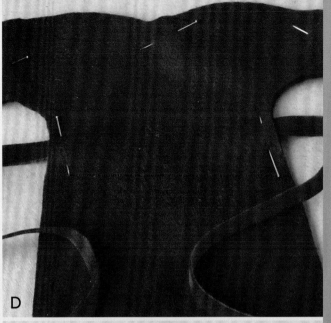

D

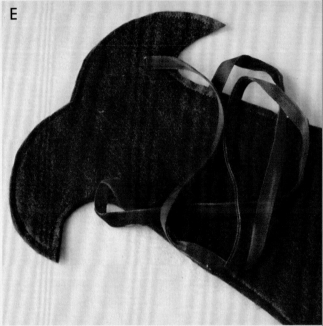

E

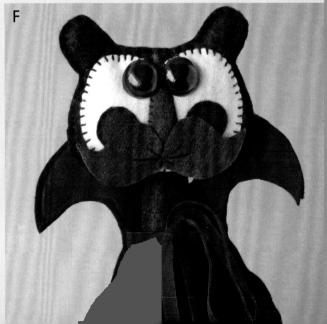

F

birthday clown bear

I realize some people don't like clowns—they think they're creepy—but I've never understood that. I can't think of anything better than a clown bear poking his snout around the door on my birthday with a big present.

All proper clowns have a pointy hat, and our clown bear has a particularly fine hat perched on one ear. He also looks slightly silly—rather ridiculous in a totally good way—a bear that makes you smile the moment you see him. The ruffle is important too, and he has a big, thick, multi-color ruffle that frames his funny face. This bear has a round tummy, which is probably because he has sampled the birthday cake before you even got to sing Happy Birthday and blow out the candles. But never fear. He is a generous soul and he has an even better cake hidden in the kitchen.

A

B

C

D

YOU WILL NEED

- Pattern templates (see pages 141, 142-143, 146, 147)
- Basic sewing kit (see pages 123-125)
- 14 x 22 in. (35 x 55 cm) gold felt for body, paws, and head
- 8 x 4 in. (20 x 10 cm) light green felt for hat and claws, and 30 x 2 in. (76 x 6 cm) for ruffle
- 5 x 4 in. (12 x 10 cm) cream felt for head front (a) and tummy, and 30 x 2 in. (76 x 6 cm) for ruffle
- 30 x 2 in. (76 x 6 cm) red felt for ruffle; scraps for cheeks
- Dark green felt for snout (scraps)
- Embroidery floss in black, red, and light green
- Yellow sewing thread
- 2 x 22 mm green safety eyes
- Sewing machine
- Red felt ball
- 2 x 5 mm black beads
- Fiberfill (toy stuffing)

METHOD

Make the body (stage one) first—see pages 38-40 for instructions, including the extra tummy stage. You should have nine felt pieces: two body and four paws in gold, one tummy in cream, and two claws in light green felt. Then go to the instructions for making the head front, here. Next, go back to the instructions on page 41 and sew the front of the head to the body. Finally, refer to page 50 for the hat and ruffle.

Head Front

1 Photocopy or trace the head pieces onto the pattern paper and cut out. You should have four pieces: head, head front, snout, cheek.

2 Pin the paper pattern pieces onto the felt. Cut out. You should have two gold heads, one cream head front, two red cheeks, and one green snout.

3 Take the cream head front (a) and position on top of the gold head front. Pin. Sew using straight stitch and black embroidery floss, see **photograph A**.

4 Position the snout on the head and pin. Sew using straight stitch and black embroidery floss, leaving a small gap for stuffing. Stuff with fiberfill, see **photograph B**.

5 Position the cheeks. Pin. Sew in place using running stitch and black embroidery floss.

6 Position the eyes on the head. Make a small hole with scissors and push the safety eye post through the hole, see **photograph C**. Push the

washer onto the post at the back of the head to secure.

7 Go to the instructions on page 41 for sewing the head back to the body. Pin the assembled head front onto the head back.

8 With a 5 mm seam allowance, stitch around the head using black embroidery floss and running stitch, see **photograph D**, leaving a gap for stuffing.

9 Stuff the head with fiberfill, then continue stitching with the black embroidery floss to close the gap.

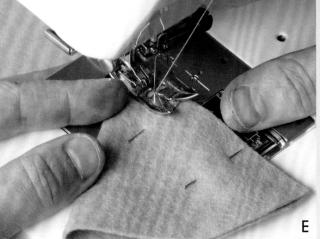

E

F

Hat

1 Photocopy or trace the hat template onto the pattern paper and cut out.

2 Pin the paper pattern piece onto the green felt. Cut out.

3 Fold the felt so that the two long cut edges are right sides facing. Stitch together using a sewing machine and pale green sewing thread, see **photograph E**. Trim the seam.

4 Turn inside out, see **photograph F**. With the red embroidery floss, bring your needle up through the top of the hat and through the felt ball. Repeat several times and secure the thread inside the hat.

5 Fold over ½ in. (1 cm) of the felt fabric into the hat inside. Pin this hem in place.

6 Using red embroidery floss and running stitch, sew around the folded hem, see **photograph G**, then secure the thread inside the hat.

7 The finished hat, see **photograph H**, will perch jauntily on one ear of your bear (see page 49).

Note: For the Santa Bear's hat, follow the instructions above, but cut out the Santa hat template twice. At Step 3 don't fold the felt shapes, instead stitch the two felt pieces together along both long cut edges, using a sewing machine and red thread. At Step 6, use white embroidery floss to sew around the folded hem.

G

H

Ruffle

1 Photocopy or trace the ruffle template onto the pattern paper and cut out.

2 Pin the paper pattern onto the green felt. Cut out. Repeat using the red felt and then the cream felt so that you have three strips of fabric.

3 Pin the ruffle pieces together with the green felt on the bottom, then the cream felt, and finally the red felt.

4 Cut three lengths of the light green embroidery floss the length of the ruffle plus 5 in. (12 cm). Thread them through a darning needle. You need to use all three strands, as otherwise the floss may break when you gather the ruffle.

5 Knot the embroidery floss and then pass the needle through a bead, see **photograph I**.

6 Begin sewing 1 in. (2 cm) from the edge of the felt, using a wide running stitch and alternating the stitches around 1 in. (2 cm) and ½ in. (1 cm) in length, see **photograph J**.

7 Start gathering the fabric as you sew, easing the three layers of felt into a ruffle.

8 Finally, place a bead onto the end of the embroidery floss and knot to secure.

9 Place the ruffle around the bear's neck and tie the two lengths of embroidery floss in a bow, see **photograph K**.

10 Trim the ends of the two lengths of floss so that they are equal, see **photograph L**. Return the ruffle to the bear's neck.

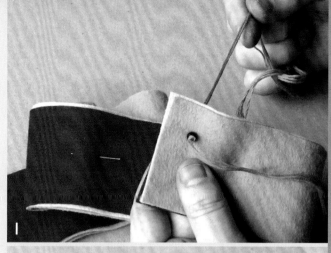

I

J

K

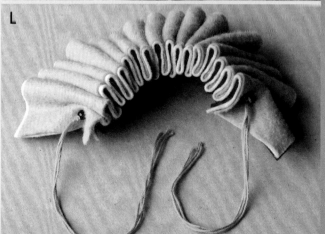

L

valentine's bear

This adorable bear is an "oooooh, awwwwh" kind of animal. In fact, when he walks through the forest that's all you hear! How can one animal melt so many hearts and make all the boy and girl bears fall in love with him?

And while he doesn't have his heart on his sleeve, he certainly has one tattooed on his arm and he is holding a big red heart just for you or the person you love. What's not to love about this bear, or for that matter any bear in the book, but a Valentine's bear must look particularly gentle and loving. You can personalize the project, too. How about stitching felt initials onto the heart or tucking a special gift under his paw? If you are giving someone a Valentine's bear, you really are saying "I love you" because a hand-made gift is always extra-special, whether you are giving it to a guy or a girl.

A

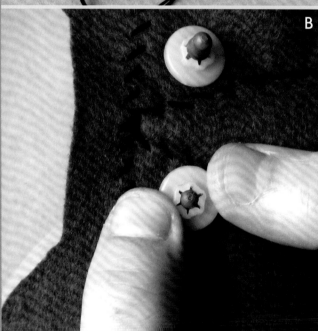

B

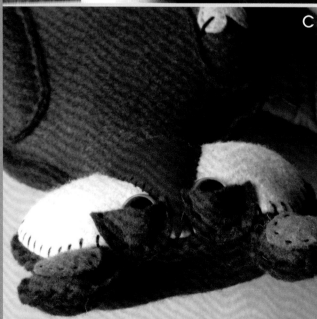

C

YOU WILL NEED

- Pattern templates (see pages 140-141, 142-143, 147)
- Basic sewing kit (see pages 123-125)
- 14 x 22 in. (35 x 55 cm) brown felt for body, paws, eyelids, and head
- Dark green felt for ear pads (scraps)
- Light green felt for tattoo (scraps)
- Off-white felt for snout (e) (scraps)
- 6 x 8 in. (15 x 20 cm) red felt for snout (d) and heart
- 5 x 4 in. (12 x 10 cm) cream felt for head front (a)
- Embroidery floss in black and white
- Brown and red sewing thread
- 2 x 12 mm blue safety eyes
- Fiberfill (toy stuffing)

METHOD

Make the body (stage one) first—see pages 38-40 for instructions, referring back here for the tattoo. You should have nine felt pieces: two body and four paws in brown, tattoo and two claws in light green felt. Once you have made the body, go to the head front instructions, below. Next, go back to the body instructions on page 41 and sew the front of the head to the body. Finally, see opposite for the heart.

Head Front

1 Photocopy or trace the templates onto pattern paper and cut out. You should have six paper pattern pieces: head (b), head front (a), inner ear, eyelid, snout (d), snout (e).

2 Pin the paper patterns onto the felt. Cut out. You should have two brown felt heads, two brown eyelids, one cream felt head front, two green felt inner ears, one red and one white felt snout piece.

3 Take the cream head front and position on top of the brown head. Pin. Using black embroidery floss and straight stitch, stitch in place.

4 Position the white snout (e) on top of the red snout (d). Pin. Sew in place using black embroidery floss and straight stitch.

5 Position the assembled snout on the head and pin. Sew in place using straight stitch and black embroidery floss, leaving a small gap for stuffing. Stuff with fiberfill, then stitch the gap closed, see **photograph A**.

6 Position the eyes on the head. Make a small hole with scissors and push the safety eye post through the hole. Push the washer onto the post at the back of the head to secure, see **photograph B**.

7 Take an eyelid and place over the right eye. Bring the needle up from the back of the work and stitch around the top of the eyelid, keeping your stitching close to the eye, see **photograph C**.

8 Tuck the end of the eyelid between the snout and eye and stitch several times to secure. This will bring the two sides of the eyelid together, see **photograph D**, and give the bear a dreamy, in-love look! Repeat with the second eyelid.

Tattoo

Pin the felt tattoo onto the top of the right paw. Sew in place using green embroidery floss and running stitch. Stitch an arrow through the heart, see **photograph E**, using the black embroidery floss.

Heart

1 Photocopy or trace the heart piece onto pattern paper and cut out. Pin the pattern piece onto the felt. Cut two.

2 Pin the heart pieces right sides together. Using red embroidery floss and running stitch, sew around the heart, leaving a gap for stuffing. Stuff with fiberfill, then sew the gap closed, see **photograph F**.

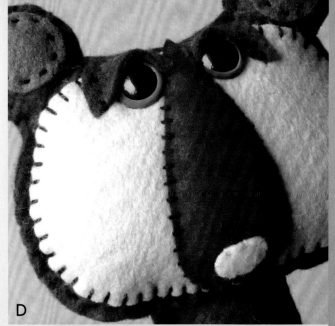

D

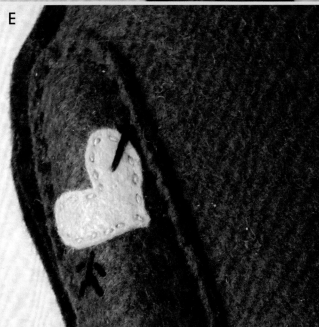

E

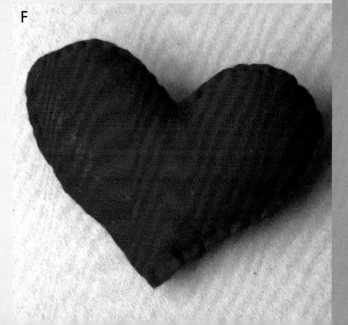

F

55

surfer bear

I sometimes call my bears by names that suit their characters and when I made Surfer Bear I called him Brad. It's a name with Californian flair and he looks the part.

He's a bear who hangs around at Woody's café on the beach listening to old Beach Boys tracks and teaching the other bears surf slang in his board shorts. In Brad's world it's all about hot-dogging (complicated surfing done by an experienced surfer bear), heavies (huge waves), and wipe-outs (a surfer bear being knocked off his board by a big wave). Brad has a retro surfboard and is very chill. You can see it in his eyes and the cut of his facial fur. His relaxed look says "beach" when other bears are saying "office," and reveals a determination never to let the summer end.

56

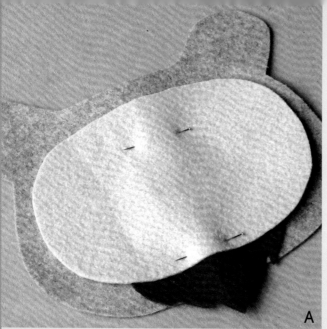

A

B

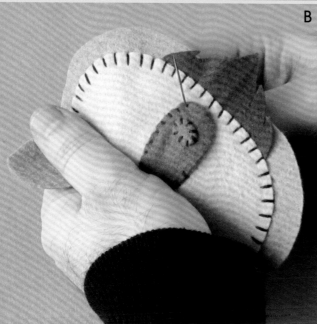

C

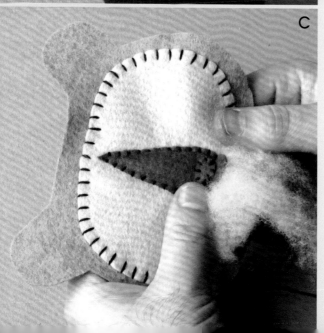

YOU WILL NEED

- Pattern templates (see pages 140-141, 142-143, 145, 146-147)
- Basic sewing kit (see pages 123-125)
- 14 x 22 in. (35 x 55 cm) blue-gray felt for body, paws, eyelids, and head
- Light green and dark green felt for snout (scraps)
- 5 x 4 in. (12 x 10 cm) cream felt for head front (a)
- Pink felt for claws (scrap)
- Brown felt for facial fur (scrap)
- 1 x 6 in. (2 x 15 cm) yellow felt for belt (scrap)
- 18 x 12 in. (45 x 30 cm) off-white felt for surfboard
- 4 x 28 in. (10 x 70 cm) red felt for shorts and surfboard
- Embroidery floss in black, red, and white
- Blue-gray and yellow sewing thread
- 2 x 12 mm green safety eyes
- Sewing machine
- 1 x 13 mm yellow glossy coconut shell button
- 16 x 5 in. (40 x 12 cm) thick cardstock and craft knife
- Fiberfill (toy stuffing)

METHOD

Make the body (stage one) first—see pages 38-40 for instructions. You should have eight felt pieces: two body and four paws in blue-gray felt and two claws in pink felt. Once you have made the body, go to the head front instructions, below. Next, go back to the body instructions on page 41 and sew the front of the head onto the body. Finally, see page 60 for instructions on how to make the shorts and page 61 for the surfboard instructions.

Head Front

1 Trace the head pieces onto pattern paper and cut out. You should have seven pieces: head front (a), head (b), snout (a), snout (b), eyelid, fur (a), fur (b).

2 Pin the pattern pieces onto the felt. Cut out. You should have nine felt pieces: two blue heads, one cream head front, two different brown fur shapes, two brown eyelids, one light green and one dark green snout.

3 Take the cream head front piece (a) and position on top of the blue-gray head. Place his beard fur (b) between the cream face and the blue-gray head, see **photograph A**. Pin. Sew in place using straight stitch and black embroidery floss.

4 Position the snout (b) on snout (a). Pin. Sew in place using black embroidery floss and straight stitch, see **photograph B**.

5 Position snout (a) on the head and pin. Sew in place using straight stitch and black embroidery floss, and leaving a small gap for stuffing. Stuff with fiberfill, see **photograph C**. Sew to complete and secure the thread on the back of the work.

6 Position the eyes on the head. Make a small hole with scissors and push the safety eye post through the hole. Push the washer onto the post at the back of the head to secure, see **photograph D**.

7 Lay the head flat on your workspace. Take an eyelid and place over the right eye. Bring the needle up from the back of the work and stitch around the top using black embroidery floss, making sure that your stitching is kept close to the top of the eyelid. Tuck the end of the eyelid between the snout and the eye and stitch several times to secure. Surfer bear's eyelids are sewn away from this safety eyes to give him his cool surfer look. Repeat for the second eyelid, see **photograph E**.

8 When you sew the back of the head onto the front (see the instructions for making up a bear's body, pages 38-40), make sure that you pin the pompadour fur (a) between his ears and the front and back of the head, see **photograph F**. Go to page 41 for attaching the head.

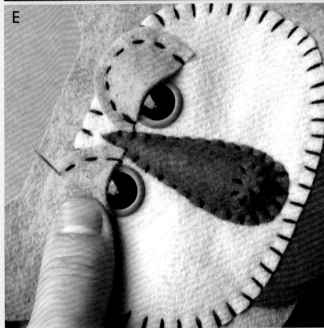
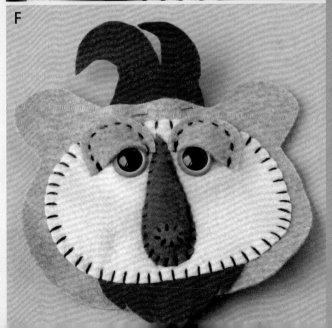

G

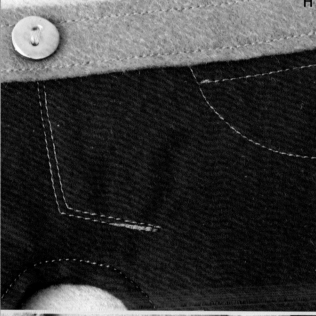

H

Shorts

1 Photocopy or trace the shorts template pieces onto the pattern paper and cut out. You should have two paper pattern pieces: shorts and belt.

2 Pin the paper pattern pieces onto the felt. Cut out. You should have three felt pieces: two red felt shorts and one yellow felt belt, see **photograph G**.

3 With a sewing machine and blue-gray sewing thread, topstitch the pocket and shorts front detailing using the photographs as a guideline.

4 Pin the belt on the shorts. Topstitch in place using a sewing machine and blue-gray thread.

5 Sew the button on the front of the shorts using yellow sewing thread.

6 Pin the back and front of the shorts with the right sides out, and leaving a seam allowance of 5 mm, sew the side seams and around the legs of the shorts using a sewing machine and blue-gray thread, see **photograph H**.

7 Gently ease the completed shorts onto your finished surfer bear, see **photograph I**.

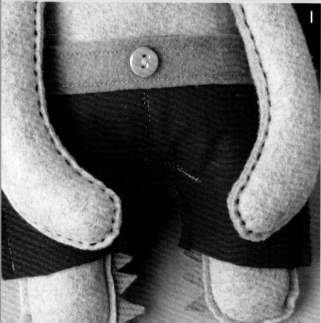

I

Surfboard

1 Photocopy or trace the surfboard template pieces onto the pattern paper and cut out. You should have two paper pattern pieces: surfboard base and top detail.

2 Pin the paper pattern pieces onto the felt. Cut out, flipping over the top detail so you get a matching pair. You should have four felt pieces: two white surfboard bases and two red top details.

3 Using a craft knife and working on a cutting mat, cut out the inside of the surfboard from thick cardstock.

4 Pin the red felt detailing onto the surfboard front and sew in place using running stitch and red embroidery floss, see **photograph J**.

5 Pin the front and the back of the surfboard either side of the cardstock. Use plenty of pins so that it doesn't move while you are sewing.

6 Leaving a 5mm seam allowance, with white embroidery floss and running stitch sew around the surfboard close to the cardstock, see **photograph K**. Secure the thread at the back of the work.

7 Tuck the finished surfboard, see **photograph L**, under your bear's paw or display it next to him.

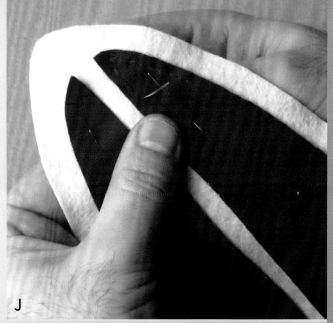

J

K

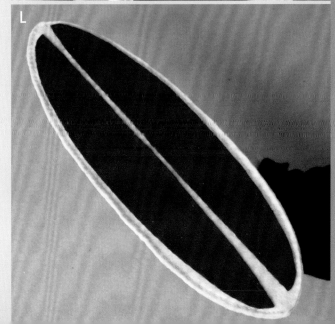

L

santa bear

When I designed this Santa bear I wanted him to look traditional but also retro, like he'd been taken out of the tissue paper in the Christmas box each year since the 1970s.

I love Christmas traditions that remind us of friends and family and if you make a festive bear I'm sure he will be part of your holiday memories—the Santa bear that visits every year for a couple of glasses of mulled wine, holding a big bag of presents in his paw. So here he is, friendly and kind with piercing blue eyes, and snug in his hat and warm gloves. He will look great sitting on a couch, perched on a shelf amid the decorations, sitting in the tree throughout the holiday season, or as the centerpice of your Christmas dinner table thinking about all the goodies he is going to eat the minute your back is turned!

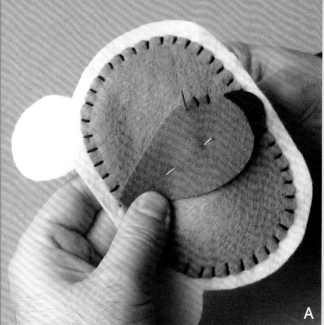

A

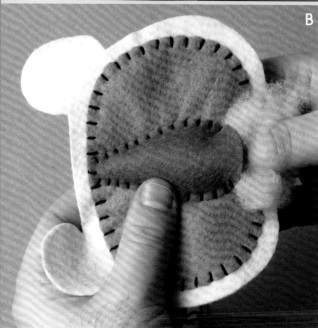

B

C

YOU WILL NEED

- Pattern templates (see pages 140-145)
- Basic sewing kit (see pages 123-125)
- 14 x 26 in. (35 x 65 mm) red felt for body, paws, cheeks, hat
- 2 x 2 in. (5 x 5 cm) yellow felt for belt buckle
- 4 x 10 in. (10 x 25 cm) black felt for gloves and belt, plus scraps for claws
- 6 x 34 in. (15 x 85 cm) off-white felt for head, eyelids, mustache
- 4 x 6 in. (10 x 15 cm) pink felt for head front
- Green felt for snout (scrap)
- 2 x 22 mm blue safety eyes
- Embroidery floss in black and white
- Red and black sewing thread
- Sewing machine
- Gray felt ball, 15 mm
- Fiberfill (toy stuffing)

METHOD

Make the body (stage one) first—see pages 38-40. You should have the following: two body pieces and four paws in red, one belt and two claws in black, and one belt buckle in yellow. Next, go to the head front instructions, below. Go back to the body instructions on page 41 and sew the head front to the body. Finally, see opposite to make the accessories.

Head Front

1 Photocopy or trace the head pieces onto pattern paper and cut out. You should have seven pieces: head front (a), head (b), head back (c), cheeks, eyelid, snout (d), mustache.

2 Pin the patterns onto the felt. Cut out. You should have nine pieces: one head, one head back, two eyelids and one mustache, all in white, one pink head front, one green snout, and two red cheeks.

3 Place the pink head on the white head front. Pin, then sew using straight stitch and black floss

4 Position the snout on the head and pin. Position the mustache below the snout and secure with a few stitches and black embroidery floss.

5 Sew around the snout using straight stitch and black embroidery floss, leaving a small gap for stuffing, see **photograph A**.

6 Stuff the snout with fiberfill, see **photograph B**. Sew the gap closed, securing thread on the back.

7 Position the cheeks. Pin. Sew using black embroidery floss and running stitch.

8 Position the eyes on the head. Make a small hole with scissors and push the safety post through the hole. Push the washer onto the post at the back of the head to secure, see **photograph C**.

9 Lay the head flat. Take an eyelid and place over the right eye. Bring the needle up from the back of the work and stitch around the top, making sure that your stitching is kept close to the top of the eyelid, see **photograph D**. Repeat with the other eye.

10 Pin the mustache between his cheeks, below his snout. Sew in place using long stitches and white embroidery floss, see **photograph E**.

Gloves

1 Trace the glove piece onto pattern paper and cut out. Pin the pattern onto the black felt. Cut four.

2 Machine sew around each glove in black thread, see **photograph F**. Don't sew across the straight top of the gloves or your bear won't be able to get his paws inside!

Hat

See page 50 for the instructions to make the hat, using red felt for the hat and a gray felt ball.

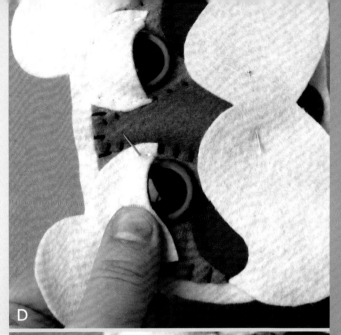

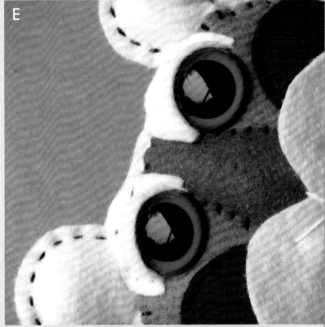

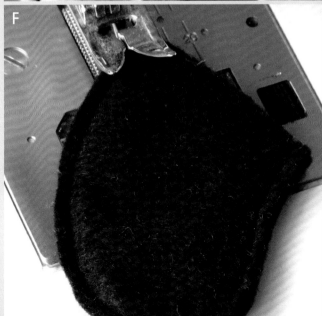

FUZZY CRAFTS

Making pictures in felt is great fun and you can either make a spring or fall scene for the bear in the forest story pillow. The pillow will look great in a modernist or traditional home, in your living room, or in the nursery, and you can change the background color to suit your interior. The best thing about this project is that you will see the fruits of your labors every day! How about making an autobearography bear for a gift, with accessories that match the hobbies of a friend? The bear shares the same body as those in the Plush Pretenders chapter, but its the extra touches that make each one so different. Or why not craft a miniature ursine mascot to keep you company on your travels?

story pillow

I love making unique and unusual things for my home. The bear in the forest story pillow looks just great on my favorite fireside chair in winter and in the summer I take it out to a sunny garden bench.

There are two stories to make—in the first, a bear strolls in the forest in fall, kicking up dry leaves and having a great time scampering under the trees in the sunlight before he returns to his cave exhausted but happy. The second is a spring scene, shown here. where the bear admires his plants in a forest clearing, with the sun on his fur making him happy to be alive. These projects aren't difficult to make, but you will need some time to cut out all the pieces and sew them in place. You might have to learn some new skills like the French knots that make the centers of the flowers, but it's worth the effort!

A

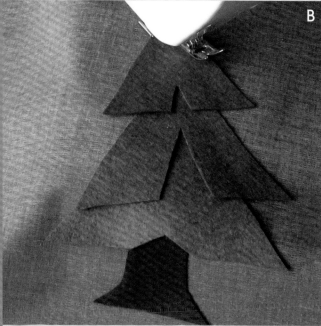

B

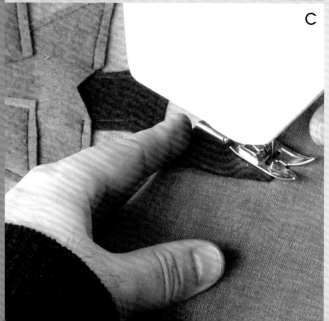

C

YOU WILL NEED

- Pattern templates (see pages 152-153, 154-155, 156)
- Basic sewing kit (see pages 123-125)
- 18 x 18 in. (45 x 45 cm) pillow form
- Gray linen fabric, 2 pieces 18 x 18 in. (45 x 45 cm)
- 6 x 12 in. (15 x 30 cm) mid-green felt for tree 1, spring leaves
- 6 x 12 in. (15 x 30 cm) dark green felt for tree 2
- 4 x 4 in. (10 x 10 cm) light green felt for tree 3
- 4 x 4 in. (10 x 10 cm) yellow felt for sun and spring flowers
- 8 x 10 in. (20 x 25 cm) dark brown felt for bear, tree trunks
- 4 x 8 in. (10 x 20 cm) rust-brown felt for spring pots or fall leaves
- Gray and black felt for snout (scraps)
- Embroidery floss in brown, orange, and yellow
- Green and brown sewing thread
- 2 x 13 mm green coconut shell buttons
- Tacky fabric glue and temporary fabric adhesive
- Sewing machine

METHOD

1 Measure and cut the two pieces of fabric for the front and back of the pillow.

2 Photocopy or trace templates onto pattern paper. Cut out. Label each piece as you go because it's easy to get confused once they're all on your work surface. You should have 17 fall or 20 spring pattern pieces.

3 Pin the pattern pieces onto the specified color felt and cut out. You should have 23 pieces for fall and 24 for the spring versions.

4 Place the felt pieces on the pillow front. Don't position any too near the fabric edge.

5 Using brown embroidery floss, sew the buttons that serve as eyes onto the bear's head, see **photograph A**. Glue the snout onto the head.

6 **Tree one/two/three:** Using temporary fabric adhesive, spray the trunk and tree pieces and stick onto the pillow front, see **photograph B**.

7 Using a sewing machine and thread to match the felt color, sew the trunk and tree pieces onto the pillow front, see **photograph C**. Start with the trunk of tree one, then the bottom tree piece, the middle, and finally the top. Next, sew the small tree three, then tree two.

Spring scene: Using temporary fabric adhesive, glue leaves, flowers, and plant pots onto the pillow front, making sure that the leaves are inside the pot. Machine sew both pot and leaves. With orange embroidery floss, sew a French knot through each flower center

Fall scene: Omit plant pots and spring flowers. Cut six rust-brown felt leaves and pin in a pile in front of the bear. Sew down the center of each leaf using brown embroidery floss and running stitch.

8 Using running stitch and brown embroidery floss, sew the bear's body and then his head onto the pillow front, see **photograph D**.

9 With yellow embroidery floss, sew the sun center onto the sun back, then sew the assembled sun in place.

10 With the pillow front and back, right sides together, using thread to match your fabric, machine sew around three sides of the pillow, leaving a ½ in. (1 cm) seam allowance.

11 Using pinking shears, trim the fabric seam to stop it fraying, then turn right sides out and stuff the pillow form into the cover, see **photograph E**.

12 Pin the gap together at the bottom of the pillow and then sew up by hand using matching thread, see **photograph F**.

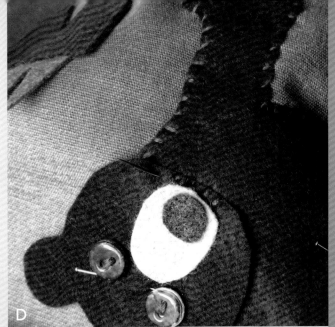

D

E

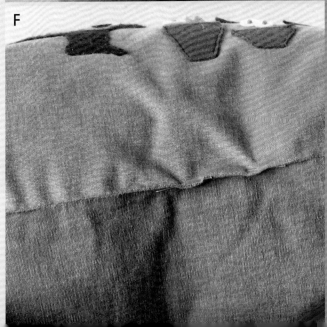

F

autobearography

I was thinking what if I make a bear that is a little bit like me? So I made some eyeglasses for my bear. And then my friend asked me to make a bear for him, with a camera because he loves taking photos.

Everybody loves a bear in their favorite color, so that's a good place to start when making a bear that's a portrait of someone. Next, think about an accessory that represents their hobby. I've made some patterns to get you started: eyeglasses, a camera, a snuggly hat, and a tasty cupcake are all easy to make and look great tucked under the paw or perched on the snout or ear. Or else get a little gift to tuck under your bear's paw. This is a project where you can let your imagination roam. I've got the ball rolling, so put on your thinking cap and make a bear that is totally unique for a special person.

A

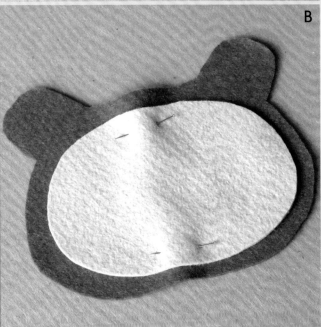

B

C

YOU WILL NEED

- Pattern templates (see pages 140-141, 142-143, 147, 150)
- Basic sewing kit (see pages 123-125)
- Fiberfill (toy stuffing)

Bear figure
- 14 x 22 in. (35 x 55 cm) green felt for body, paws, eyelids, and head
- Red felt for snout (scraps)
- 6 x 4 in. (15 x 10 cm) cream felt for head front and claws
- Black embroidery floss
- 2 x 12 mm silver safety eyes

Camera
- 4 x 4 in. (10 x 10 cm) black felt for camera body and lens
- 2½ x 2½ in. (6 x 6 cm) white felt for lens outer ring
- Black and red embroidery floss
- 2 x 13 mm red glossy coconut shell buttons
- 1 x 16 mm safety eye
- 16 in. (40 cm) striped cotton ribbon

Eyeglasses
- 4 x 4 in. (10 x 10 cm) yellow felt
- Thin, clear cellophane
- Black embroidery floss

Hat
- 8 x 4 in. (20 x 10 cm) red felt
- Cream embroidery floss
- Red felt ball

Cupcake
- 6 x 4 in. (15 x 10 cm) pink felt for cake top
- Red felt for cherry (scraps)
- Green felt for cherry stalk (scraps)
- 4 x 8 in. (10 x 20 cm) cream felt for cake
- Black embroidery floss

METHOD

1 Photocopy or trace off the pattern pieces onto pattern paper. You should have seven figure pieces: head front (a), head (b), body, claw, snout (d), eyelid, paw. Cut out the paper patterns.

2 Pin the paper patterns onto the felt in your chosen colors (see list on oppostie page) and cut out, see **photograph A**.

3 See the instructions for making a bear's body on pages 38-40. Follow the instructions up to making the head front.

4 Use the instructions below to make the head, then return to the instructions on page 41 to complete the bear's head.

Head Front

1 Take the cream head front (a) and position on top of the green head. Pin, see **photograph B**. Sew the head front in place using straight stitch and black embroidery floss.

2 Position the snout on the head front and pin. Sew in place using straight stitch and black embroidery floss, leaving a small gap. Stuff with fiberfill, see **photograph C**. Finish stitching.

3 Position the eyes on the head front. Make a small hole with scissors and push the safety eye post through the hole. Push the washer onto post at the back of the head to secure, see **photograph D**.

4 Take an eyelid and place over the right eye, see **photograph E**. Bring a needle threaded with black floss up from the back of the work and stitch around the top of the eyelid, making sure that your stitching is close to the edge. Tuck the end of the eyelid between the snout and the eye and stitch several times to secure. Repeat, see **photograph F**.

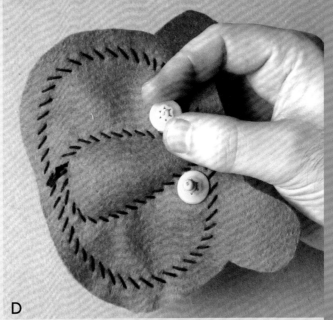

D

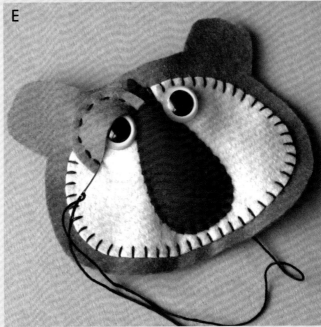

E

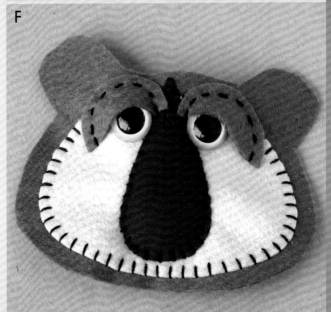

F

G

H

I

J

Camera

1 Pin the paper pattern pieces onto the felt. Cut out. You should have four pieces: camera front, camera back, and lens center in black felt, and a white felt outer lens ring.

2 Sew the black lens centerpiece onto the white lens outer ring piece using running stitch and red embroidery floss.

3 Sew the two red shell buttons onto the camera front using the red embroidery floss.

4 Sew the assembled lens onto the camera front using running stitch and red embroidery floss, see **photograph G**.

5 Make a small hole with scissors in the middle of the lens and push the safety eye post through the hole, see **photograph H**. Push the washer onto the post at the back of the work to secure.

6 Pin the camera front and back together, sandwiching the striped ribbon between the front and back in the position shown in **photograph I** to make the camera strap.

7 Sew the camera front and back together using running stitch and black embroidery floss, leaving a gap for stuffing. Stuff the camera body with fiberfill, see **photograph J**, then continue stitching to close the gap; knot the thread to secure. The camera is ready to hang around your bear's neck!

Eyeglasses

1 Pin the paper pattern piece onto the yellow felt. Cut out two pieces, see **photograph K**.

2 Place the felt pieces on either side of the sheet of thin, clear cellophane, and pin, see **photograph L**.

3 Stitch the felt and cellophane sandwich together using running stitch and black embroidery floss, making two longer stitches across the bridge of the eyeglasses, see **photograph M**.

4 Cut the cellophane around the eyeglasses close to the felt. Perch the eyeglasses on the bear's nose and secure with a stitch or two.

Hat

1 Pin the paper pattern piece onto the red felt. Cut out one piece.

2 Follow the instructions for making a hat on page 50, skipping the step for the felt ball.

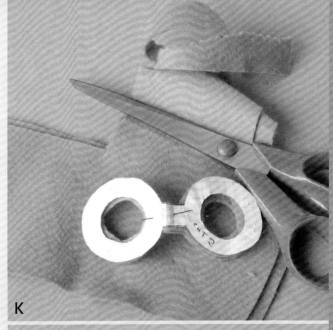

K

L

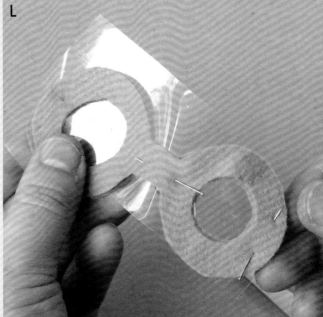

A camera-toting autobearography bear, ready to set off on his world travels.

M

77

Baking fan or simply greedy? This delicious cherry cupcake is
the perfect accessory—just make sure that the recipient doesn't
eat it!

Cupcake

1 Photocopy or trace off the pattern pieces onto pattern paper. You should have 4 pieces: cupcake, cupcake top, green stalk, red cherry. Cut out the paper patterns.

2 Pin the paper pattern pieces onto the felt. Cut out. You should have six pieces: cream cupcake front, cream cupcake back, pink cupcake top, red cherry front, red cherry back, and green cherry stalk.

3 Place the pink cupcake top and the cherry back on the cupcake back, see **photograph N**.

4 Using black embroidery floss, sew through the three fabrics using small stitches in the middle of the cherry to secure. Don't sew too near the top as you will need to sew around the whole cupcake at a later stage.

5 Using black embroidery floss, sew the front and the back of the cherry together, with the stalk placed between the two pieces of fabric, see **photograph O**. At the top you are just sewing the cherry. At the bottom you are sewing the cherry onto the cupcake.

6 Sew across the bottom of the cupcake top using running stitch and black embroidery floss, see **photograph P**.

7 Sew the cupcake bottom detail using a long straight stitch and black embroidery floss. Sew over the long stitch with a smaller stitch to secure.

8 Leaving a 5 mm seam allowance, sew the cupake front and back together using running stitch and black embroidery floss, and leaving a gap for stuffing. Stuff with fiberfill. Stitch the gap closed, knotting the thread to secure, see **photograph Q**.

N

O

P

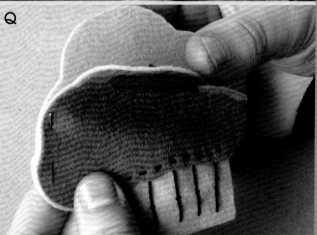

Q

mini mascot bear

I do a lot of traveling and sometimes I need a friendly bear to keep me company on the road, either hanging out in my campervan or safely tucked into my bag.

So here's mascot bear, cheery and bright when you are feeling tired after a day on the road or smiling in the morning when you start your day in a strange place. I've put a loop at the top of his head so that you can hang him up. Sometimes all we need is to keep a happy little bear in our sights to make the day, and our travels, go just right. You can make this project smaller if you want an even more miniature bear. Not too small, though, or he will get lost (and be a bit difficult to make, too). Small is good in my book, and a miniature bear, or even a whole family, to keep me company seems just right.

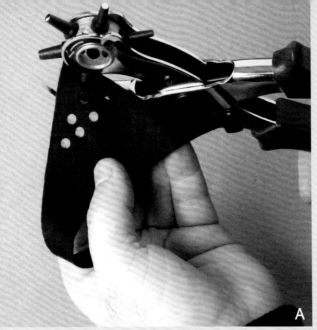

A

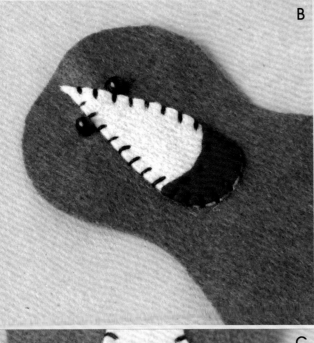

B

C

YOU WILL NEED

- Pattern templates (see page 149)
- Basic sewing kit (see pages 123-125)
- 6 x 10 in. (15 x 25 cm) green felt for the body, paws, ears
- Orange felt for the bow tie (scraps)
- Blue felt for the knot (scraps)
- Red felt and cream felt for the snout (scraps)
- Pink felt for the ear center (scraps)
- Black felt for the paw pads (scraps)
- Hole punch
- Black embroidery floss
- 2 x 5 mm black beads, for eyes
- 8 in. (20 cm) of striped cotton ribbon
- Fiberfill (toy stuffing)

METHOD

1 Photocopy or trace the bear mascot pattern pieces onto the pattern paper and cut out. You should have eight paper pieces: body, snout (a), snout (b), ear, inner ear, bow tie, bow tie knot, paw.

2 Pin the paper pattern pieces onto the felt. Cut out. You should have 16 felt pieces: two body pieces, four ears and four paws in green, one orange bow tie, one blue tie knot, one red and one cream snout, and two pink felt inner ears.

3 Cut the pads from a piece of black felt using the hole punch, see **photograph A**.

4 Position the snout (a and b) onto the head and pin. Sew in place using straight stitch and black embroidery floss.

5 Sew the black bead eyes onto the head using black thread, see **photograph B**.

6 Sew a mouth pattern onto the head using the embroidery floss and straight stitch.

7 Pin, then sew the bowtie and knot pieces onto the body by making a cross with the stitches in the middle of the knot, see **photograph C**.

8 Sew the ear pad onto the ear front using a small straight stitch and black embroidery floss. Repeat for the second ear.

9 Sew the front and the back of the ear together using a running stitch and black embroidery floss. Repeat the process for the second ear.

10 Sew the paw pads onto the front paw pieces with a small stitch, see **photograph D**. Repeat. Then sew the front and the back of the paw together using a running stitch and black embroidery floss, leaving the top of the paw open for stuffing.

11 Repeat step 10 with the second paw, then fill both paws with fiberfill.

12 Pin the front and the back of the body together, placing the paws, ears, and ribbon between the two pieces in the correct positions, see the pattern template and **photograph E**.

13 Sew around the bear's body using black embroidery floss and a running stitch. When you have a small gap left, fill the bear with fiberfill, see **photograph F**.

14 Complete the sewing to close the gap, and finish off with a small neat knot.

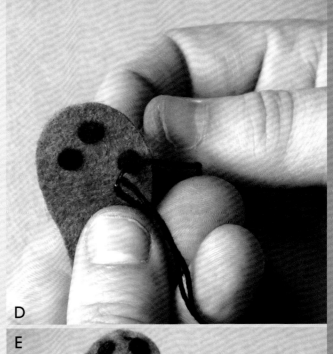

D

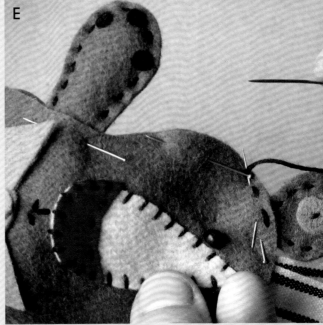

E

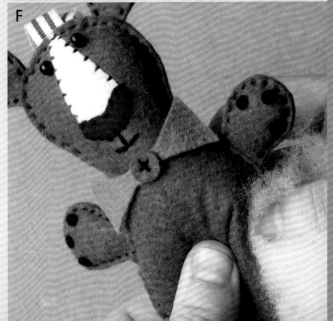

F

CUDDLY CLOTHING

Dress up, bear style, top to toe! Start by snuggling up toasty warm in a fuzzy woolen bear scarflette that hugs your neck. I have made a polar bear version, but don't let this stunt your creativity as it would look great in brown, as a grizzly scarflette, or black, for a black bear version, or even in black and white, panda style. You must know how to knit to make the scarflette, but don't let this worry you as simple knitting stitches will give you wonderful results. The scarflette looks good on men, women, and kids—although I admit that you'll need a certain style to pull it off as an adult! Then thread some superchic bears through your laces to bring urban cool to your kicks—these decorations are really easy to make.

polar bear scarflette

When fall turns to winter my thoughts turn to wooly scarves. I want to be toasty warm but look great too. I came across a polar bear picture in a book, and despite the ice he looked so snuggly that I began designing a scarflette!

The scarflette is a bit of fun, but it looks very good too as the knitting creates a big white fuzzy collar. I've made the project in an adult size, and it looks great on men and women, but you can make the knitting slightly shorter for a kid's size. It's not a scarf, so the polar bear face should sit just below the chin.

One final thing. You don't need to be a super-skilled knitter to make this project. If you can cast on and off and knit and purl then you are ready to go. The combination of stitches I've used is a bit forgiving too, so if you go slightly wrong and get your purl and your knit mixed up don't worry, folks won't notice at all.

A

B

C

YOU WILL NEED

- Pattern templates (see pages 151, 152-153, 154)
- Basic sewing kit (see pages 123-125)
- 2 x 100 g balls of Rowan Tumble (90 percent alpaca, 10 percent cotton) yarn
- White fineweight knitting yarn, small amount, for finishing
- Knitter's pins and yarn needle
- 2 x size 17 knitting needles
- 18 x 22 in. (45 x 55 cm) white 100 percent wool felt
- 7 x 16 in. (15 x 40 cm) thick muslin or canvas
- White embroidery floss
- 2 x 9 mm safety eyes
- Large covered hook and eye
- Fiberfill (toy stuffing)

METHOD
Knitted Section

If you are new to knitting, refer to a tutorial in a book or video for instructions—or get a friend to teach you.

Cast on 39 stitches, see **photograph A**.

Work the following pattern until the piece measures approximately 26 in. (65 cm):

Row 1 (Right side) *Knit 3, Purl 1, repeat from * to last 3 stitches, Knit 3.
Row 2 Knit 1, Purl 1, Knit 1, * Knit 2, Purl 1, Knit 1, repeat from *

Cast off in rib, see **photograph B**. Trim and weave in any loose ends.

Fold the knitting in half so that the seam will be in the middle of the back of the work (not to one side as it will be too bulky), see **photograph C**. Pin, then measure against the felt pieces; if necessary adjust seam allowance. Sew together using white yarn. Don't use the yarn you knitted with as it is too bulky!

Polar Bear Head and Paws

Next, make the felt head and paws—these will be attached one each end of your knitted section.

1 Photocopy or trace the polar bear scarflette pattern pieces onto the pattern paper and cut out. You should have six paper pieces: head (a), head back (b), snout (a), snout (b), paw (a), paw (b).

2 Pin the paper pattern pieces onto the felt. Cut out. You should have six felt pieces: one head front (a), one head back (b), one snout (a), one snout (b), one paw (a), and one paw (b).

3 Pin the head (a) and paw (a) paper pattern pieces onto the muslin. Cut out. You should have two muslin pieces, one to line the head and one (with a central hole) for the paw lining, see **photograph D**.

4 Cut around the muslin pieces with pinking shears, making sure that they are slightly smaller than the felt pieces, see **photograph E**.

5 Pin felt snout piece (b) onto felt snout piece (a) and stitch in place using straight stitch and white embroidery floss.

6 Sew the assembled felt snout onto the felt head front (a) using straight stitch and white embroidery floss.

7 Position the safety eyes on the head. Make a small hole with scissors and push the safety eye post through the hole. Push the washer onto the post at the back of the head front piece to secure, see **photograph F**.

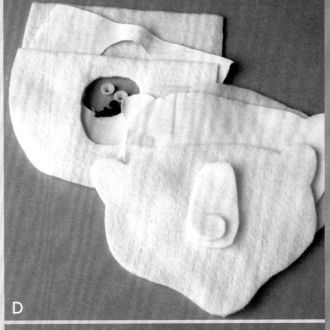

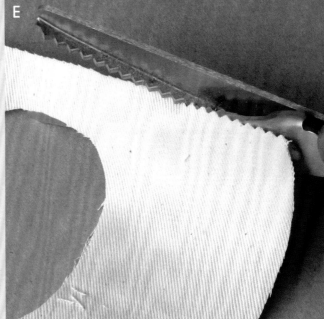

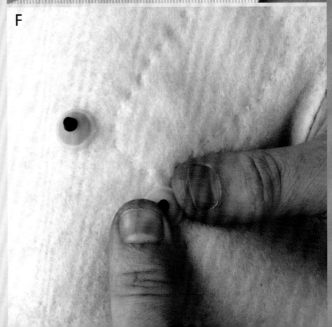

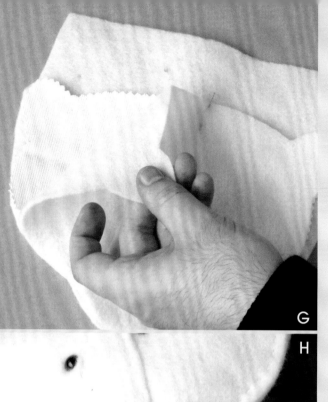

G

H

I

8 Pin the felt head front (a) and head back (b) together with the muslin head lining sandwiched between the two pieces, see **photograph G**. This interlining helps the felt head keep its shape.

9 Leaving a 5 mm seam allowance, sew around the head using white embroidery floss and a running stitch, and leaving a small gap for stuffing. Make sure that you catch the muslin piece with your stitches as you sew so that it cannot move.

10 Stuff the head with fiberfill, see **photograph H**. Finish sewing the head pieces together to close the gap and knot the thread to finish.

11 Pin the felt paws (a) and paws (b) together, with the muslin paw lining sandwiched between the two felt pieces, see **photograph I**.

12 Sew around the outside edge and then the inside edge of the paw using white embroidery floss and a running stitch. Again, make sure that you catch the muslin with your stitches so that it cannot move.

13 Position the top part of the felt head into the middle of the front knitted part of the scarflette, with the seam at the center back. Pin using knitting pins, see **photograph J**. Make sure that the knitting is as close to the top of the ears as possible and in a straight line on both sides of the work.

14 Sew the head to the knitted section using the white embroidery floss. Make sure that the stitches go over each loop of the knitting. Don't split the yarn by stitching in between the strands of a knitted stitch or make really big stitches that would create a gap, otherwise your scarflette won't be strong enough to wear!

15 Now repeat with the paws. Position the top part of the paw into the middle of the front knitted part of the other end of the scarflette, with the seam at the center back. Pin using knitting pins. Make sure that the knitting is in a straight line on both sides of the work.

16 Sew the paw to the knitted section using the white embroidery floss, taking care that the stitches go over each loop of the knitting. Don't split the yarn or make really big stitches.

17 Put your scarflette on and see how much overlap of the paws and the head you need in order to wear it comfortably. Pin the hook to the back of the head and the eye to the front of the paw. Stitch the hook and eye in place using the white embroidery floss, see **photograph K.**

Care advice: Your scarflette should stay looking good for a long time, see **photograph L,** but you could always dry clean if necessary.

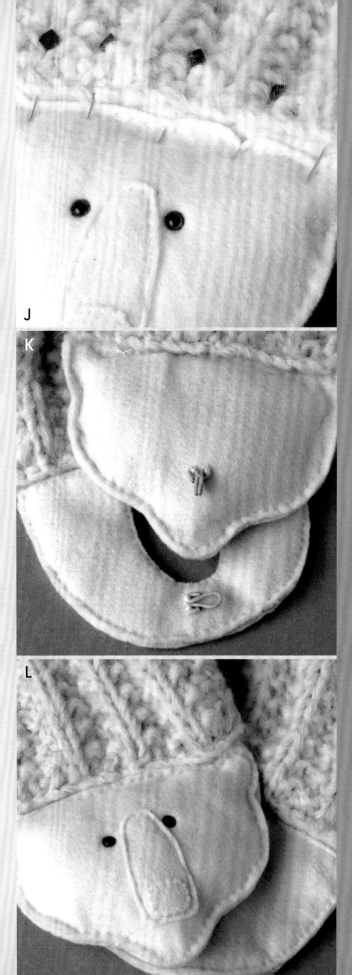

J

K

L

bear laces

I love quirky street style. In a city where anything goes, however weird and wonderful your clothes are, folks will laugh with you, not at you. So I've designed some beary fun for funky high tops.

These little bear heads are super-simple to make and they're a project that you can tuck into your bag and pull out when you have a few moments for crafting. I have a couple of tips: make sure that you use strong, clear plastic for the stiffeners, and if the bears get wet, dry them rightaway! My boot bears have padded their way through an urban winter and their eyes are still shining bright. I love the way they make people smile every time they look down at my high tops. They are a great way of starting conversations with fellow crafty folk—and making others laugh too!

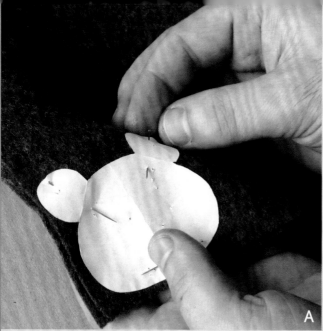

A

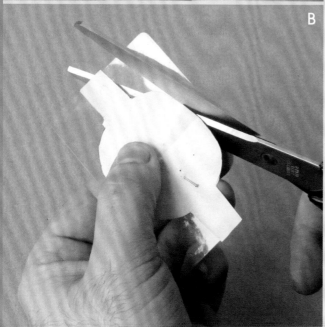

B

YOU WILL NEED

- Pattern templates (see page 158)
- Basic sewing kit (see pages 123-125)
- 6 x 6 in. (15 x 15 cm) blue felt for head (a)
- 6 x 6 in. (15 x 15 cm) pink felt for head (b)
- Red felt for the snout (scraps)
- 6 x 4 in. (15 x 10 cm) thick, clear plastic
- Craft knife or scissors
- Hole punch
- Black embroidery floss
- Black sewing thread
- 4 x 5 mm black plastic beads

METHOD

Note: You are making two bears. Repeat means do the same thing again to make the second bear!

1 Photocopy or trace the patterns onto the pattern paper and cut out. You should have four pattern pieces: head (a), head front (b), snout, stiffener strip.

2 Pin the paper patterns for the head and snout onto the felt, see **photograph A**. Cut out. Repeat. You should have four heads (a) in blue felt, two head fronts (b) in pink felt, and two red felt snouts.

C

3 Place the stiffener strip pattern onto the plastic and pin (it doesn't matter about the pinholes as they will be covered by the felt). Cut out with scissors or a craft knife, depending on the thickness of your plastic, see **photograph B**. Use a hole punch to make the holes on the ends for the laces. Repeat.

4 Sew the pink head front (b) onto the blue head (a), using the black embroidery floss. Repeat.

5 Sew the red snout onto the head using the black embroidery floss. Repeat.

6 Using black sewing thread, sew the black plastic beads that form the eyes onto the head. Repeat.

7 Place the back of the head, the plastic and the front of the head together and pin.

8 Sew around the head in running stitch and black embroidery floss, see **photograph C**. Repeat.

9 Undo the laces of your sneakers until they are about halfway undone. Thread the bears onto the laces then re-lace to the top.

URSINE ACCESSORIES

I love making complicated things. Some of the projects in this book will take you a couple of days to make. But there are other times when I want to make simple projects which I can create in a matter of minutes or an hour. The projects in this chapter are very easy to make and would be great as gifts or, of course, as a present for yourself! All of these projects are rather crazy, and I make no excuse for that. Sometimes you want to stand out from the crowd, have fun, go full-on— and I've called that the glamour bear look! So here we go: dress up in wild rings, look-at-me earrings, and mad-as-a-hatter headbands or you can make a cute cell phone cover. They are all sure to get you noticed and show that you love bears.

you look great!

My friends' kids love dressing up and rings and earrings are their favorite accessories. It took me only a little time to make this fantastic bear bling!

Sometimes you need some instant craft and here it is: a set of bear-face earrings and a ring. I've made these in my favorite retro 1970s color combination of orange and pink, but you can create your own color scheme—say, browns or a forest-toned green—and they will look just as good. The earring project is great if you want to keep younger people happy making things. Maybe the bear outlines won't be so neat, but who cares. There is something so good about making stuff when you are a kid (I was bitten by the design-and-make bug when I was very young). These easy projects hold the attention and you'll get almost instant results. The ring is a bit more fussy to make, but it is a fun bear bling dress-up, and makes a wonderful party favor too, so it's worth the extra effort.

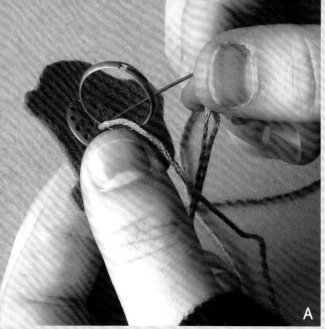

A

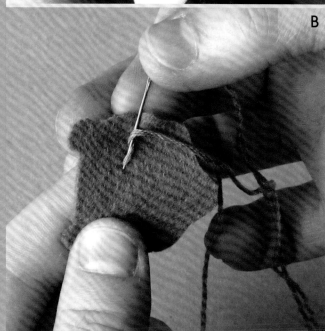

B

C

YOU WILL NEED
- Pattern template (see page 157)
- Basic sewing kit (see pages 123-125)

Bear ring
- Pink felt (scraps)
- Craft ring back
- Embroidery floss in pink and orange
- Fiberfill (toy stuffing)

Earring
- Orange and red felt (scraps)
- Hole punch
- Hoop earrings

METHOD
Ring

1 Trace or photocopy the pattern template onto the pattern paper and cut out.

2 Pin the paper pattern piece onto the pink felt and cut out two bear heads.

3 Sew one of the bear heads onto the craft ring back using the pink embroidery floss. Make sure that the ring back is in the middle of the head, see **photograph A**.

4 Take the other bear head and sew two French knots for eyes using pink embroidery floss, see **photograph B**.

5 Place the two bear heads together and blanket stitch around the edge using orange embroidery floss, see **photograph C**. When you have just a small gap left, push some fiberfill between the heads—just enough to make the heads slightly padded.

6 Continue to blanket stitch around the head until you have closed the gap.

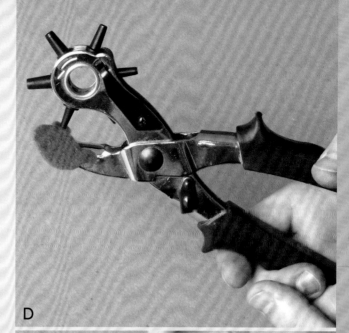

D

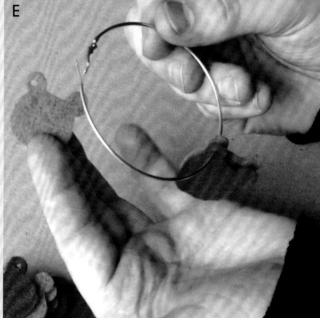

E

Earrings

1 Trace or photocopy the pattern template onto the pattern paper and cut out.

2 Pin the paper pattern onto the orange felt and cut out seven bear heads.

3 Pin the paper pattern onto the red felt and cut out six bear heads. If you like, you can cut out more bears so that the whole ring is threaded with bears!

4 Turn the hole punch so that it is set to the smallest hole it produces.

5 Punch a hole in the middle of the ear of each bear, see **photograph D**.

6 Thread the bears onto the ring, see **photograph E**, starting and finishing with an orange bear!

7 Repeat the instructions from step 2 in order to make a second earring in the same way, see **photograph F**. Now you have a pair!

F

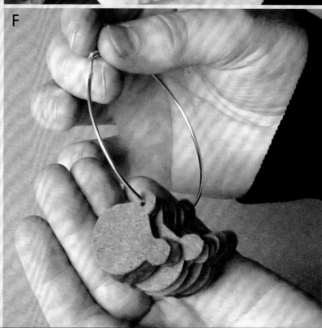

101

bear pin

A felt pin is a cute starter project. Entry-level bear fun, it's an ideal way of using up felt scraps leftover from other projects and no one is going to send the bear police around if the colors get a little crazy.

I've chosen a natural color combination, but you can also try sunshine colors or neon brights. I find that once you have made one it's difficult to stop, not only because I love making these hot accessories but because people keep asking me if I will make one for them, and their friend, and their friend's friend. ....Whoa! It's tough to call a halt to all this pinmaking with the hordes banging on the door asking me to make more and more. You will find that these bear pins look great on a coat, but they are big enough to stick on your bag for some super-high-energy bear power.

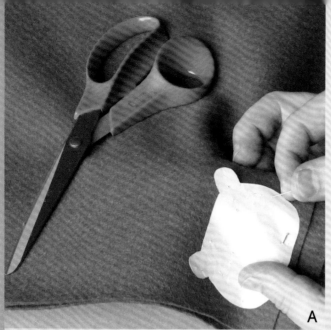

A

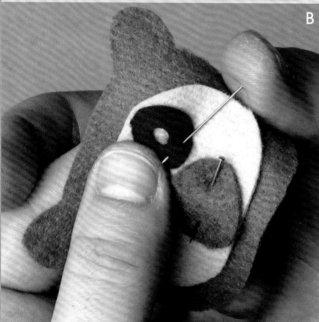

B

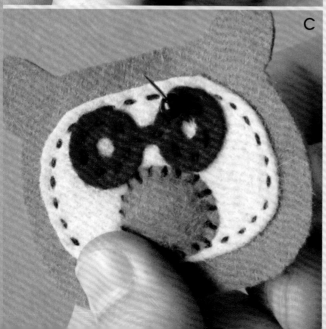

C

YOU WILL NEED

- Pattern template (see page 158)
- Basic sewing kit (see pages 123-125)
- 4 x 6 in. (10 x 20 cm) green felt for head (a)
- 4 x 4 in. (10 x 10 cm) cream felt for head front (b)
- Light blue felt for snout (scraps)
- Red felt for eyeglasses (scraps)
- Black embroidery floss
- Black sewing thread
- 2 x 5 mm black beads
- Fiberfill (toy stuffing)
- 1 x pin back

METHOD

1 Photocopy or trace the pattern pieces onto the pattern paper and cut out. You should have four pieces: head (a), head front (b), snout, eyeglasses.

2 Pin the paper pattern pieces onto the felt, see **photograph A**. Cut out. You will have five felt pieces: two green heads, one cream head front, one blue snout, and one red pair of eyeglasses.

3 Sew head front (b) onto head (a) using running stitch and black embroidery floss.

4 Position the eyeglasses and the snout pieces onto the head front and pin, see **photograph B**. Once you are happy with the expression, use black embroidery floss to sew them in place using running stitch for the eyeglasses and straight stitch for the snout. Secure the thread on the reverse to finish.

5 Position the beads that serve as eyes onto the head. Sew in place using black sewing thread, see **photograph C**.

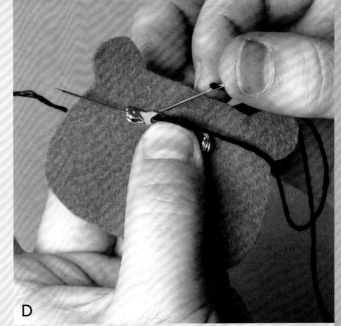

D

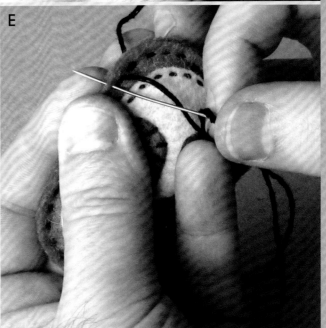

E

6 Using black sewing thread, sew the pin back on the bear head, near the top of the second head piece (the back), see **photograph D**.

7 Pin the two bear heads together, right sides out. Sew using running stitch and black embroidery floss, see **photograph E**.

8 When you have a small gap left, fill the bear's head with fiberfill, see **photograph F**. Complete the sewing and finish off and knot the thread.

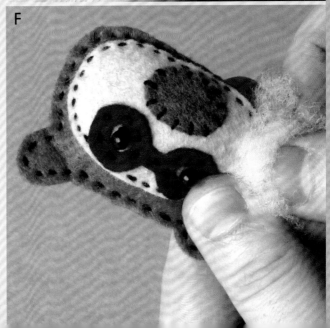

F

head bear hairbands

I had kids in mind when I designed this project, but these bear headbands are popular with all ages, from schoolgirls to party girls to moms!

I get inspiration from all over the place. I was looking at photos of my sisters when we were kids in the 1980s and they were wearing hairbands. My mind clicked over like clockwork, and I came up with this design. The big surprise is that these bear headbands are loved by people of all ages and they can look either really girly or nightclub cool depending on who is wearing them. Easy to make, these hairbands use up leftovers from other projects. Don't forget to knot the elastic when you make this project, otherwise it has a habit of untying and then—ping—there goes your bear like a catapult! Not a good look.

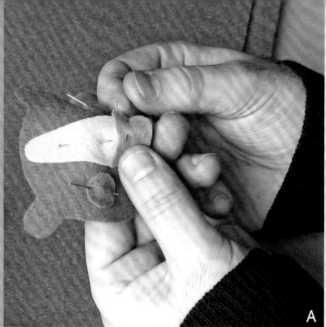

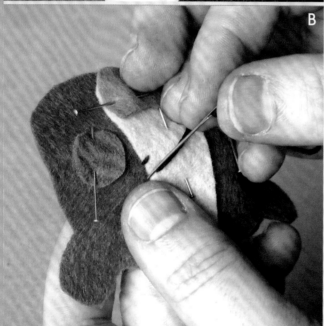

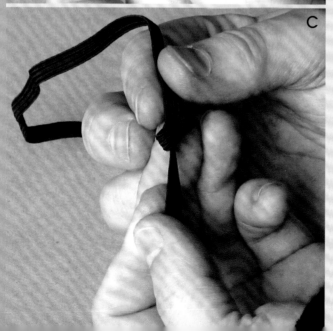

YOU WILL NEED

- Pattern templates (see page 148)
- Basic sewing kit (see pages 123-125)
- Scraps of felt in the colors of your choice. You will need four colors for each headband you make: one color for the head, one for the snout (a), one for the snout (b), and one for the cheeks. You will only need small pieces, so this is a great project for using up scraps
- Black embroidery floss
- Black sewing thread
- 2 x small round black beads
- 20 in. (53 cm) thin black elastic
- Fiberfill (toy stuffing)

METHOD

1 Trace or photocopy the bear hairband pattern pieces onto the pattern paper and cut out. You should have four pattern pieces: head, snout (a), snout (b), cheek.

2 Pin the paper pattern pieces onto the felt and cut out. You will have six felt pieces in the colors of your choice: two heads, one large and one small snout, and two cheeks.

3 Position the cheeks on the head and pin. Position the snout pieces (a and b) onto the head and pin, see **photograph A**.

4 Sew the bear's features in place using straight stitch and black embroidery floss, see **photograph B**.

5 Using black embroidery floss, sew one stitch in the middle of each cheek to secure to the head.

6 Position the beads that form the eyes on the head. Once you are happy with the expression, stitch in place with black sewing thread and secure the thread on the reverse to finish.

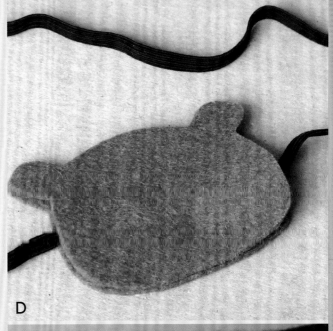

D

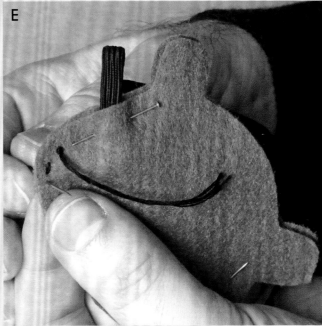

E

7 Put the elastic around your head to make sure that you have the right length. You will need to allow an extra 1 in. (2.5 cm) to sew the ends into the bear's head. I suggest that you try 20 in. (50 cm), which fits most heads. Once you are happy with the length, knot each end, see **photograph C**. The knots preserve the tension the elastic is under, preventing it from untying loose.

8 Pin the two bear heads together, with the right sides out and the knotted elastic ends sandwiched in between the heads just below the ears, see **photograph D**.

9 Using black embroidery floss, sew around the head using running stitch, leaving a small gap for stuffing. Make sure that you securely catch the elastic into each side of the bear's head, see **photograph E**.

10 Fill the bear's head with fiberfill. Don't fill it too much. Complete the sewing to close the gap, and finish off with a small, neat knot, see **photograph F**.

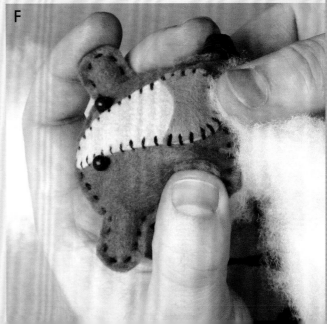

F

cell phone cover

The cases that are available for cell phones are so boring, and I wanted to design something that was much more fun. So what do we have here? Why, it's a retro business bear in his cool bowtie.

The project uses thick wool felt because you need to protect your phone as well as making it look cool. The blanket stitch edging is hardwearing, too, and will withstand lots of pulling and tugging as you get your phone out or put it away. Make sure that you measure your phone so that you get the right size. If you are making this as a present then be aware that some folks would find this cover too bright (don't you hate it when you make a present and then it's not used, grrrr!), so if you think that's the case then make it in monochrome black and white or in more muted shades. It will look just as good.

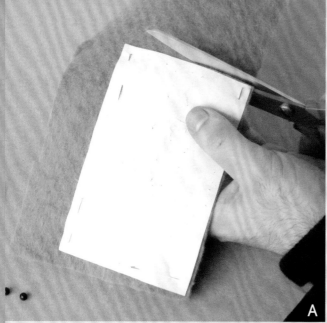

A

YOU WILL NEED

- Pattern templates (see pages 148, 149)
- Basic sewing kit (see pages 123-125)
- 8 x 6 in. (20 x 15 cm) thick green 100 percent wool felt
- Red felt for the bowtie (scraps)
- 2 x 2 in. (5 x 5 cm) blue felt for the head (scraps)
- Cream and red felt scraps for the snout
- Black embroidery floss
- Black sewing thread
- 2 x 5 mm black plastic beads
- 1 yellow coconut shell button

METHOD

1 Trace or photocopy the pattern pieces onto the pattern paper and cut out. You should have five pieces: head, snout (a), snout (b), bowtie, cover.

2 Pin the paper pattern pieces onto the felt. Cut out, see **photograph A**. You should have six felt pieces: two green covers, one red bowtie and snout, one white snout, and one blue head.

3 Position the cream and red snout (a and b) pieces onto the head and pin.

4 Sew the snout to the head using straight stitch and black embroidery floss, see **photograph B**.

5 Sew the black plastic beads that act as eyes onto the head using black sewing thread, see **photograph C**.

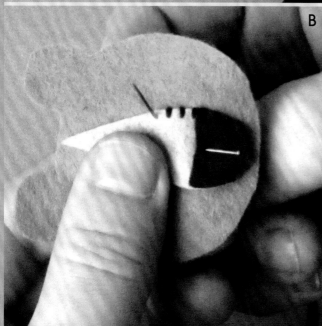

B

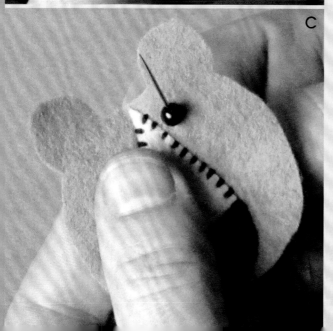

C

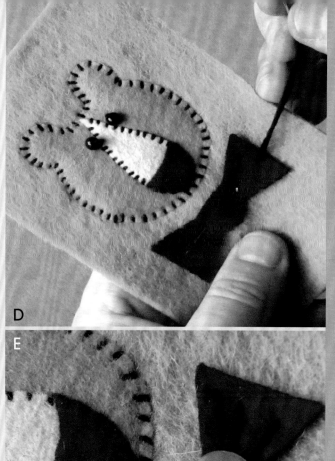

D

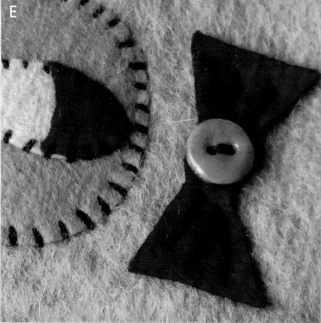

E

6 Pin, then sew the blue felt head onto the front of the cover using a straight stitch and black embroidery floss.

7 Pin, then sew the bowtie onto the front of the cover using long stitches and black embroidery floss, see **photograph D**.

8 Sew the yellow coconut shell button into the middle of the bowtie using black sewing thread, see **photograph E**.

9 Pin the wrong sides of the front and back cover together and sew around three sides using blanket stitch and black embroidery floss, see **photograph F**.

F

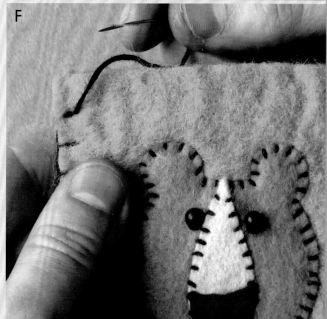

113

stuff sack

I love stuff sacks. It's great making order out of chaos, and with my baseball bear stuff sack I can tuck all of my sports stuff or school stuff or crafting stuff out of sight and neat.

This canvas stuff sack features a baseball-playing bear. You can adapt the design by taking the pattern for one of the other bear's heads and sewing it onto the front, or you could use the bear head design from the earrings and sew little bears all over! Or how about using the Santa head to make a Santa sack for Christmas presents? There are lots of other ideas too. Maybe you'd like to stitch the vampire head onto a sack for trick-or-treat candy or the camera-toting autobearography bear onto a bag for your camera accessories? If the stuff sack isn't big enough, then you can size up the pattern.

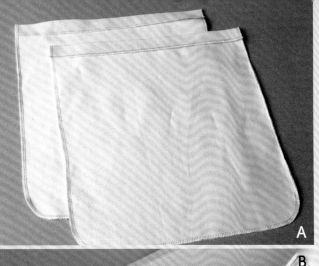

A

B

C

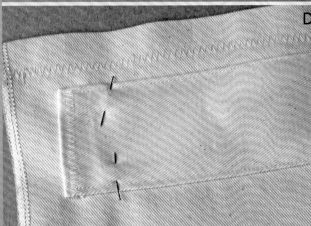

D

YOU WILL NEED

- Pattern templates (see pages 156-157)
- Basic sewing kit (see pages 123-125)
- 21 in. x 36 in. (52 cm x 90 cm) wide canvas
- Sewing machine with overlock stitch; iron
- Length of cord, 3 yds (2.4 m), cut into two
- Brown felt for bear's head and bat (scraps)
- Red felt for bear's body (scraps)
- Off-white felt for ball (scraps)
- Embroidery floss in black and yellow
- Sewing thread to match the bag fabric

METHOD

1 Cut two pieces of canvas 14 x 17 in. (35 x 42 cm) and two pieces 12 x 3½ in. (32 x 9 cm).

2 On the large pieces of canvas, round off two of the corners, see **photograph A**. Press.

3 Serge/overlock all the edges of the canvas pieces to stop them fraying.

4 Turn over 1½ in. (3 cm) at the top of both large pieces (the bag front and back). Press.

5 Turn over 1½ in. (1.5 cm) seam allowance around the small canvas pieces (the cord guides). Trim the corners. Press, see **photograph B**.

6 Sew the hem on the short side of each cord guide using a zigzag stitch, see **photograph C**.

7 Pin cord guides to sack pieces 1½ in. (3 cm) from top and 1½ in. (3 cm) from each side, see **photograph D**, with the right side of the sack front and the wrong side of the cord guide together. Pin.

8 Machine sew cord guides onto the sack along the long sides. Don't sew short sides of the guide otherwise you won't be able to thread in the cord!

9 Machine sew a line along the middle of each cord guide to create two parallel channels.

10 Photocopy or trace off the pattern templates. You should have five pieces: head, snout, body, bat, ball. Pin the paper patterns onto the felt and cut out. You will have five felt pieces.

11 Hand sew the snout onto the head using straight stitch and black embroidery floss.

12 Make two eyes using French knots and yellow embroidery floss, see **photograph E**.

13 Using straight stitch and black embroidery floss, sew the bear's body onto the sack in your chosen position. Make sure that you don't sew it too close to the edge of the sack, see **photograph F**.

14 Next, using straight stitch and black embroidery floss, sew the bear's head onto the body, then the bat, and then the ball, creating the curved stitch lines on the ball.

15 Place the two sack pieces right sides together and machine sew around the sides and bottom, leaving a ½ in. (15 mm) seam allowance, see **photograph G**. Turn right sides out.

16 Secure one of the two pieces of cord to a long, thin knitting needle using sticky tape. Thread through the cord guide. Repeat with the second cord length, but starting at the gap opposite.

17 Knot the cord ends. If your cord is fraying at the cut edges, use some clear craft glue to secure the cord end.

18 Pull the cord loops in opposite directions to gather the top, see **photograph H**. Your sack is ready to use!

F

G

H

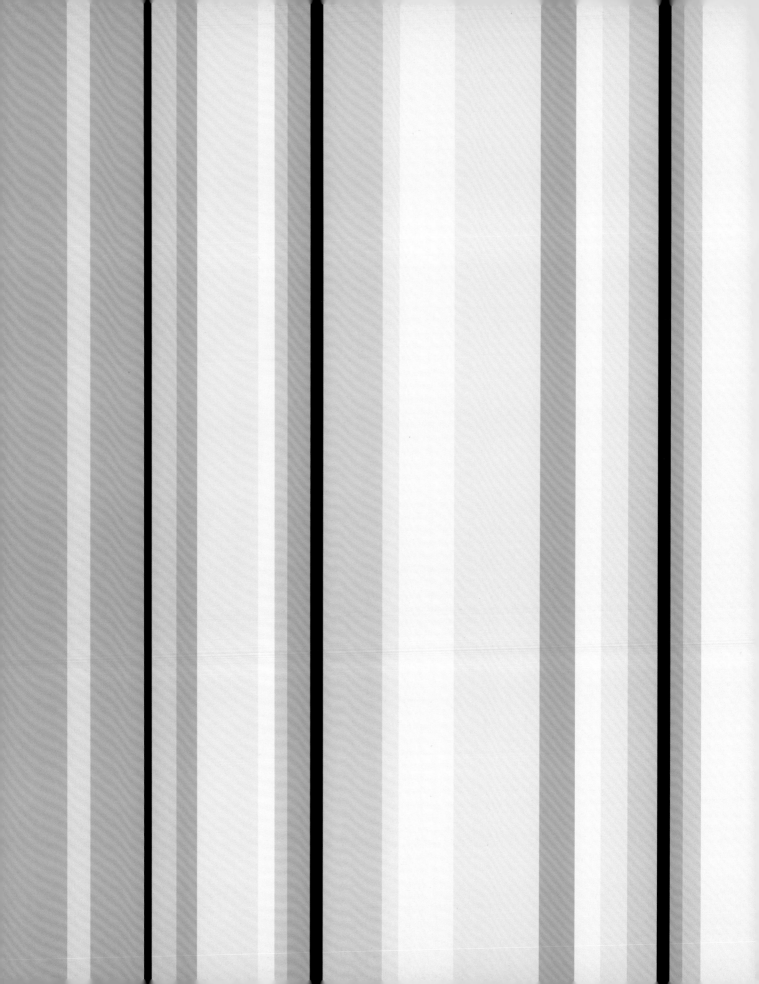

BEAR NECESSITIES

There really is nothing too complicated about the techniques I've used to make the projects in this book, but sometimes we all need a little help and this chapter is here to provide just that. So if you need extra information to make a project, then look here first. There is a quick guide that will show you how to choose the right tools and materials, and some useful extra hints and tips on crafting techniques. Before starting a project, it's a good idea to go through all the supplies you need. There is nothing worse than finding out that you don't have a vital component to finish your project and you have to put down tools for a few days until you can get to the store or your online order reaches you.

material tips

All the materials you need to make the projects in this book can be obtained from a good craft store, but I use the Internet for most of my supplies, mainly because I love receiving a small package of craft goods through the mail!

Pattern paper

I often use dressmaker's pattern paper as the grids and lines are useful to center a pattern, but it's really not necessary. In the photographs for this book I used ordinary plain 11 x 17 in. drawing paper—this is available in pads and it works just fine.

Tracing paper

If you don't have access to a photocopier to copy the patterns, you can use tracing paper to trace them. Tracing paper is available in single sheets or pads from art shops and suppliers.

Pencil and sharpener

An ordinary HB pencil works well for most projects. You need to keep your pencils nice and sharp—I usually use a craft knife for this, but a pencil sharpener will work just as well.

Felt fabric

Almost all the projects in this book use felt. In most cases the bears are made from an easy-to-find, inexpensive, standard-weight 100 percent synthetic felt, and if that is all that you can get then don't despair. If you choose the colors carefully everything will be fine. I use felt with a higher percentage of wool. Although this type is difficult to find and much more expensive, it's well worth the effort if your local craft store can obtain it for you or if you can order it online. Both types are available in squares of various sizes and by the yard/meter which is more economical for large projects. I have chosen felt colors that I think work well together, but the bear projects can be made in any color combination you like. If you make several of the larger projects in the book you will have plenty of scraps leftover that you can use for some of the smaller projects, such as the pin or the earrings.

The polar bear project uses 100 percent wool felt. Wool felt is not as robust as the wool/synthetic mix type, but it is super-fluffy and it comes in a beautifully gentle white.

The cell phone cover project uses a bulkier felt, which is around ¼ in. (7 mm) thick. You can obtain this in squares that are just big enough to make the phone project.

Felt balls

Ready-made felt balls are available in ½, ¾, and 1¼ in. (1, 2, and 3 cm) sizes—I use ¾ in. (2 cm). A wide range of colors are available online.

Embroidery floss

I use cotton embroidery floss and cut around a 23½ in. (60 cm) length to sew with, as I find that if I use a piece any longer than this, the thread tangles. If you run out, then simply knot and start with a new length of thread.

Sewing thread

Use cotton/polyester thread for sewing on buttons and bead eyes and machine sewing. Don't buy the very cheap thread that can be

bought in bulk. The quality is usually poor and the colors harsh. In my opinion it's worth spending the extra on Coats, Gutermann, or another good branded thread.

Fiberfill (toy stuffing)

Synthetic toy stuffing is clean, easily available and works well with all the projects. In the past, people used all sorts of odd things to stuff dolls—such as old tights, teeshirts or towels—and the results were variable. My advice is don't do it—it's well worth spending a little on purpose-designed stuffing. I tend to stuff the bears so that they are rigid and this gives a solid, sculptural effect. However, you can use less stuffing and make a softer animal; it's simply a matter of taste.

Muslin/canvas

The scarflette lining and the stuff sack base are both made from muslin fabric. Muslin comes in different weights, from a fine, almost muslin-like material to a thick, tough fabric. Medium to thick muslin is what you need for both of these projects; alternatively you can use a medium-weight canvas.

Ribbon, elastic and cord

Part of the fun of crafting is choosing your materials. I have suggested some ribbon, elastic, and cord types and my preferred colors for these choices in each of the project's You Will Need listings, but feel free to vary the colors and materials—making sure that whatever you select will work with the project of course!

Cellophane

The eyeglasses for the Autobearography project have clear cellophane for their "lenses." I don't buy this, but simply recycle it from discarded packaging I have on hand in my studio.

Temporary fabric adhesive spray

For the Story pillow project, you will need a temporary fabric adhesive in spray form. You spray the adhesive onto the back of the applique fabric piece and then you can position and reposition it until you get the placement just right. Another advantage of this method is that you can then machine-sew the pieces in place without the bother of adding and then removing pins that can pucker and distort the felt. Follow the manufacturer's instructions and make sure that you use this spray in a well-ventilated room.

Craft glue

I use Crafter's Pick Incredibly Tacky Craft Glue, a non-toxic, all-purpose glue. I've tried every kind of glue on the market, and in my opinion this is the best.

Cardstock

I used a standard 0.05 in. (1.4 mm) thick sheet mounting board for the Sloth Bear Bookmark project.

Jewelry findings

I use metal pin and ring backs designed for craft use; these are easily available. I suggest you don't use the very cheap jewelry findings as they break easily. Who wants to invest time in making a project only to find it broken after its first wearing?

Safety eyes

The size of the safety eyes is mentioned in each project and should be followed, although you can vary the color. They are available through craft suppliers and if you are making several projects then they can be bought in bulk too.

Beads

If you are using beads for eyes, make sure that the projects are not given to small children.

your toolkit

You don't need complicated equipment to make the projects in this book, but you will need some basic tools. Not all the projects need the full kit, so if you want to get started super-quick just get the basics and choose an easy project from the Ursine Accessories chapter to get started.

BASIC KIT

Some people love collecting lots of gadgets. I have two mottos in life and I also apply these to my designing and making. The first is to keep things as simple as possible. Why complicate things when it's not necessary? The second is to buy the best you can afford—cheap types are never a pleasure to use and always breaks just at a crucial moment. So with those two thoughts informing my choices, here are some suggestions for basic kit.

Scissors

Buy a good pair of dressmaking scissors, also embroidery scissors and a pair of pinking shears. My mom is still using the dressmaking scissors she bought in the 1970s, and if yours last that long you can see that the initial small investment is worth the money. You will also need a separate set of paper-cutting scissors for your pattern templates. With all three scissors, you will be set up for all your crafting fabric projects for life.

Tip: Keep your sewing scissors well away from paper, because it blunts them. Make a band from a scrap of felt to color-code the handles if your sewing scissors look too similar to your paper ones.

Needles

A lot of projects in the book require hand sewing with embroidery floss. You don't need a special needle for sewing the felt, but make sure that you buy one with a large enough head to be able to thread the floss through.

Word of warning: Don't use a super-thick needle—sometimes labeled as a tapestry needle—as it will be hard to pull through the felt.

Pins

You can never have too many pins, starting with a good box of steel dressmaker's pins.

Tip: Make a pincushion from some old fabric and they will always be to hand. I made up the bear pin project on pages 102-105 and just left off the pin back so I've a beary pincushion!

ADDITIONAL TOOLS
Self-healing mat

These cutting mats are great for any project—they will protect your tabletop from damage by sharp scissors and pins and they have the extra advantage that they make accurate cutting very simple since they have a grid printed on the plastic surface. I purchased my first self-healing mat a few years ago. It's laid out on my workspace all the time and I can cut, pin, and even stand the sewing machine on it, and it bounces back as good as new. Another great thing about these mats is that if you don't have a permanent studio you can easily move your work around from room to room. Just make sure that you buy the largest size that fits comfortably on top of your sewing table.

Sewing machine

A good sewing machine was one of the best investments I made. You don't need a complicated machine. In fact, I've made all the projects in the book on my home machine, rather than my commercial machine, to make sure that they are easy to produce at home. All you need is a sewing machine that creates a basic straight stitch, a zigzag, and an overlock (it's sometimes called serge, and it stops the fabric from fraying).

Iron

Felt doesn't respond well to steam irons. The hot, moist steam can destroy the fabric and leave a strange textured finish all over your project. Most projects don't need pressing, but if they do, then you should use a simple dry iron with a pressing cloth between the iron and the felt to protect it.

Knitting needles

There's only one project in the book that includes knitting. If you choose to make the polar bear scarflette on pages 86-91 you will need to buy a pair of needles in size 17 US. I love using wooden knitting needles. I've even got some vintage needles in a beautiful polished wood, but while it will make your project nicer to achieve it won't make the slightest difference to the quality of the knitting. My advice? Buy plastic and ask for wood as a lovely Christmas or birthday present!

Knitter's pins

When I made up the polar bear scarflette I used knitter's pins to secure the strip of knitting to the felt ends. You can see them in the instructional photographs on page 91. They are thicker than dressmaker's pins, and have colored heads so that you can find them in the knitting and they don't split the yarn. They are not strictly necessary, but they are a good item to invest in if you make up knitted projects regularly.

Metal ruler/French curve

As a craft maker/designer and a man, I really don't understand tape measures. They give you the wrong measurement if they fold up slightly. They are fine for dressmaking, but for bear making I have taken the metal ruler from my workshop and it works well. I suggest you do the same. The French curve is a useful dressmaking tool, however, and I wouldn't be without one as it's see-through and makes some projects much easier to achieve.

Craft hole punch

These are sometimes call leather hole punches and have a ring at the top so that you can vary the size of the hole used. My advice is when you are buying a hole punch is to make sure that the smallest hole size is, well, small.

Tip: Always clear cut bits of fabric or cardstock away from the punch as soon as possible, otherwise it won't work as well.

Craft knife

There are hundreds of different craft knives out there, and I'm sure they are all equally good. My advice is to buy one with a retractable blade and make sure that you have a good stock of replacement blades or that you can buy them easily nearby—because a blunt or uncomfortable craft knife is a nightmare.

Fine hacksaw

You can buy a fine-toothed hacksaw, sometimes called a Junior Hacksaw, in any craft store. They usually come with a selection of blades for use on wood and metal. You will need to use the hacksaw to cut the skewer that reinforces the giant panda's bamboo branch.

Starter kit: 1 Craft mat **2** Knitting needles **3** Knitter's pins **4** French curves **5** Craft knife **6** Needles **7** Pin cushion **8** Pinking shears **9** Dressmaking scissors **10** Embroidery scissors.

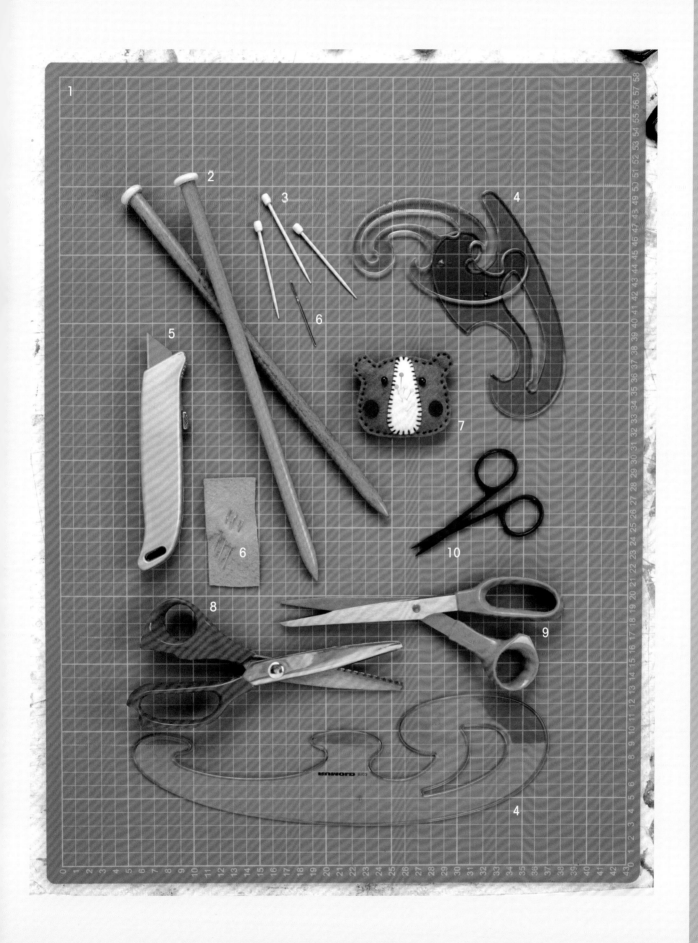

technique tips

All the projects in this book are easy to make and you don't need any special sewing skills. In this section you will find advice on copying the patterns and instructions for the stitches.

Photocopying or tracing the patterns

There are several methods you can use to make the patterns for the projects. The easiest way is to photocopy the book pages onto regular copier paper. All the patterns are reproduced at 100 percent, so there is no need to set any enlargement on your machine, except for the Polar Bear which is at 93 percent. You can even scale up the patterns on a photocopier if you want to make any of the projects a little larger than the originals. Once you have made your photocopies, just cut carefully around the template outlines and there are your paper patterns ready to use.

Another way to create the paper patterns is to trace the templates onto pattern paper which is thin enough to see through. This is the method I use because it is simple to do at home if you don't have a copier to hand, and when you are working with the resulting paper patterns it's easy to keep the patterns straight using the graph paper lines as a guide. Once again, just cut around the outline to make your patterns.

Hand sewing and machine sewing

Many of the projects in the book use both hand sewing and machine sewing. I love hand sewing because it makes projects portable. If you have a spare moment, you can pull the project out of a plastic bag (to keep it super-clean) and spend your time crafting. You can make most of the projects just using a sewing machine instead of hand stitching, and it will be far quicker. They will look slightly different, but just as good!

French knot

These little knots are useful for making eyes or flowers.

1 Knot one end of a length of embroidery floss and bring the needle and floss through from the reverse of the work to the right side of the fabric, see **photograph A**.

2 Hold the length of floss taut at all times. Place the needle in front of the floss and wrap the floss around the needle twice, see **photograph B**. When you wrap the floss around the needle keep the needle steady—don't be tempted to twist it.

3 Re-insert the needle very close to, but not in exactly the same spot as, the place where your length of floss came out from the fabric. Just to remind you again, keep it taut so that, as the needle goes through the fabric, the little bundle of floss slides up the needle, see **photograph C**.

4 Give the needle a final tug and it will slide through to the wrong side of the work, leaving a tiny French knot on the right side, see **photograph D**.

It went wrong? Don't worry, practice makes perfect, so try it again. The most common problem with making a French knot is not keeping the floss taut throughout the stitch and then it all unravels.

A

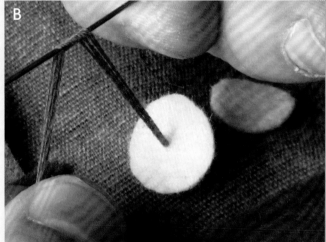

B

C

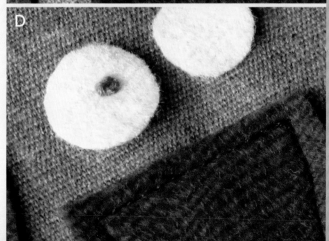

D

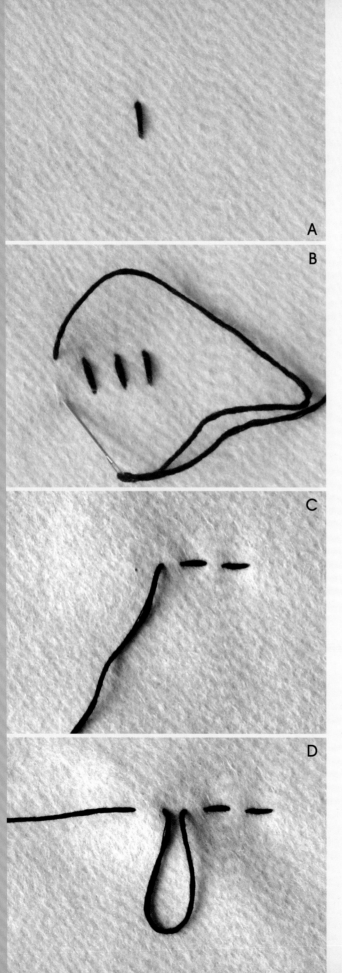

A

B

C

D

Straight stitch

This is a very simple stitch that looks a bit like blanket stitch, but without the top loops.

1 Knot one end of the thread or floss you are using and, starting on the reverse of the work, bring the needle and thread through to the right side.

2 Re-insert the needle about ¼ in. (5 mm) from the place where your thread came out from the fabric and pull the needle through to the wrong side of the work, see **photograph A**.

3 Carry the thread along the back of the work about 5 mm farther and then bring the needle back through to the right side again so that it emerges next to the base of the first stitch and ¼ in. (5 mm) along, see **photograph B**. Repeat steps 2 and 3 as needed.

Running stitch

This is a very simple stitch that creates what looks like a little line of dashes along your work.

1 Knot one end of the thread or floss you are using and, starting on the reverse of the work, bring the needle and thread through to the right side.

2 Re-insert the needle ⅛ in. (2 mm) farther along and pull the needle through to the wrong side of the work.

3 Carry the thread along the back of the work ⅛ in. (2 mm), then bring the needle back through to the right side again, see **photograph C**.

4 Try to keep all of the stitches the same length because this will look neater, see **photograph D**.

Blanket stitch

This versatile edging stitch is used to join the two halves of the cell phone cover project.

1 Knot one end of the thread or floss you are using and, starting on the reverse of the work, bring the needle and thread through to the right side, see **photograph E**.

2 Take the needle through the fabric at right angles to the original thread, see **photograph F**.

3 Make sure the thread is looped under the needle, see **photograph G**.

4 Pull the needle through so that the thread forms an L shape, see **photograph H**. Continue until you have completed the number of stitches required for the project.

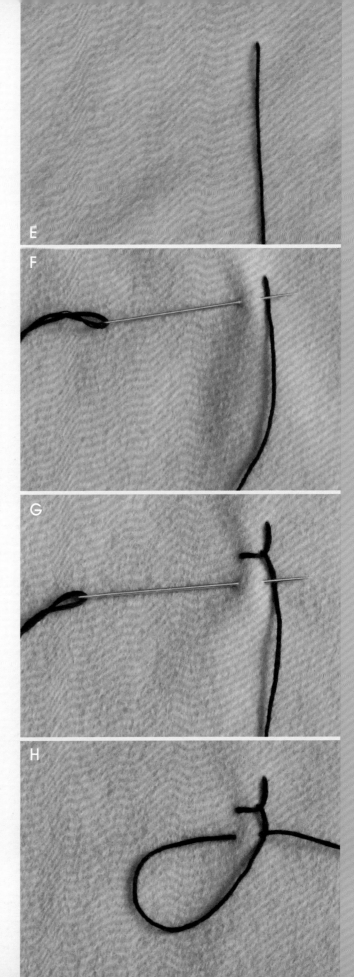

E

F

G

H

129

TEMPLATES

Check the list of template pieces you will need in the instructions for your chosen bear, then identify them in this chapter and photocopy or trace the ones you need onto plain paper or dressmaker's pattern paper. If you are going to make any of these projects several times, it's worth copying the templates onto a thick cardstock instead. All the templates shown here, apart from the Polar Bear and the Grizzly Bear, are the same size as the ones I drew to make the bears for the book, so you can simply copy them directly. It's a good idea to make all the templates you need for your chosen projects before you start cutting out any pieces so that you can lay them out to make the most economical use of your felt fabric.

really beary templates

The first section of this chapter provides all the templates for the projects based on real bears in the Really Beary chapter on pages 10-33.

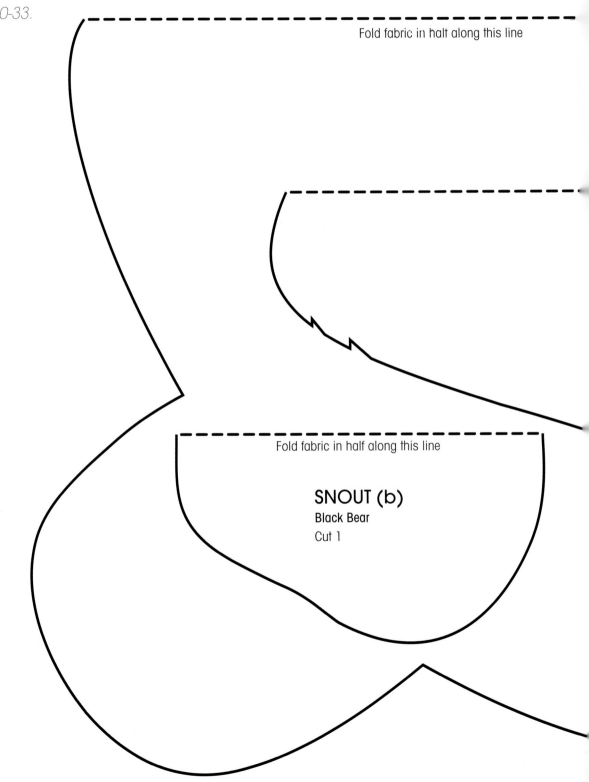

Fold fabric in halt along this line

Fold fabric in half along this line

SNOUT (b)
Black Bear
Cut 1

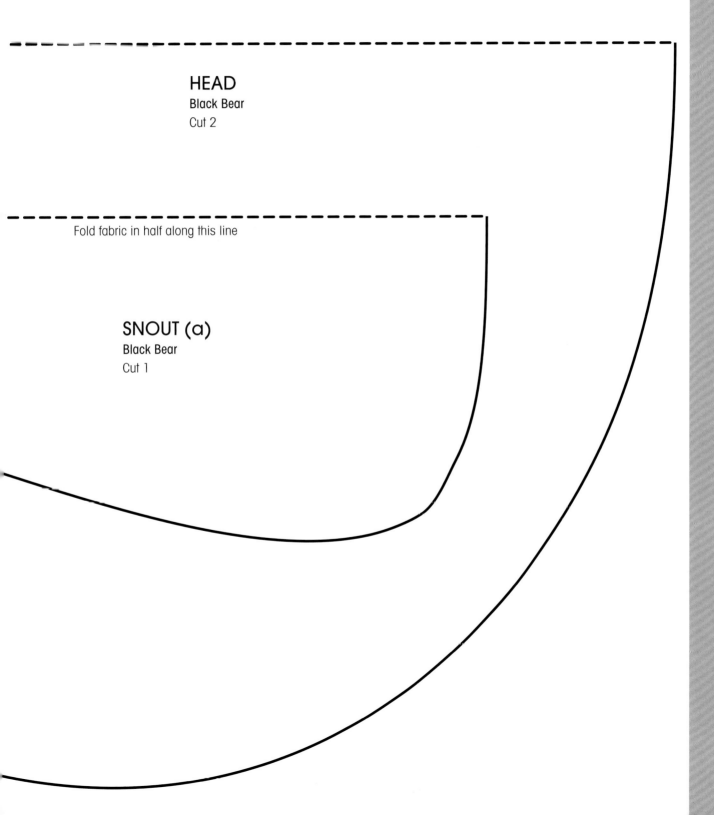

HEAD
Black Bear
Cut 2

Fold fabric in half along this line

SNOUT (a)
Black Bear
Cut 1

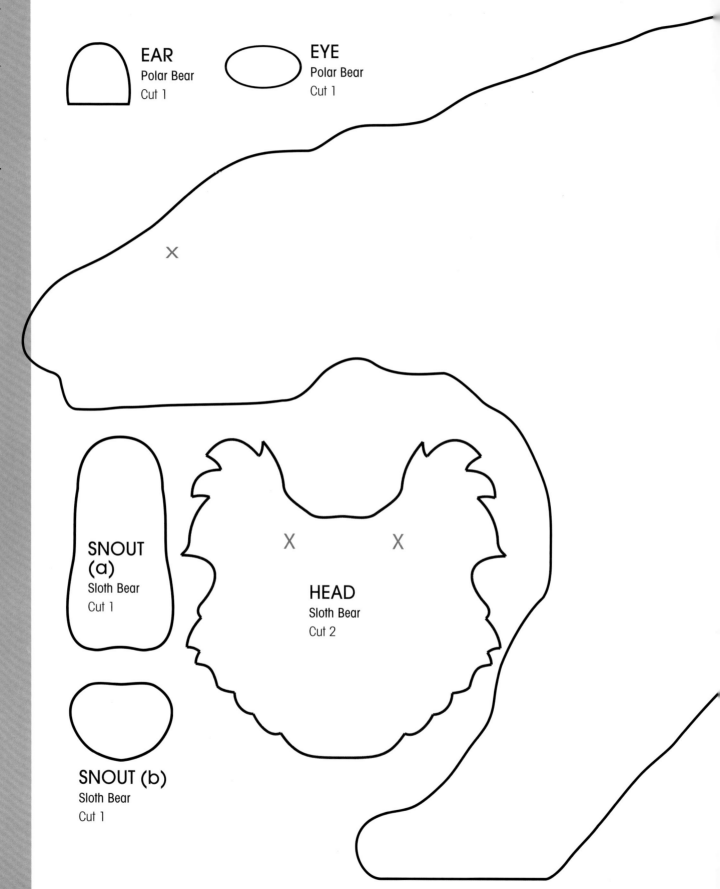

EAR
Polar Bear
Cut 1

EYE
Polar Bear
Cut 1

X

SNOUT
(a)
Sloth Bear
Cut 1

X   X

HEAD
Sloth Bear
Cut 2

SNOUT (b)
Sloth Bear
Cut 1

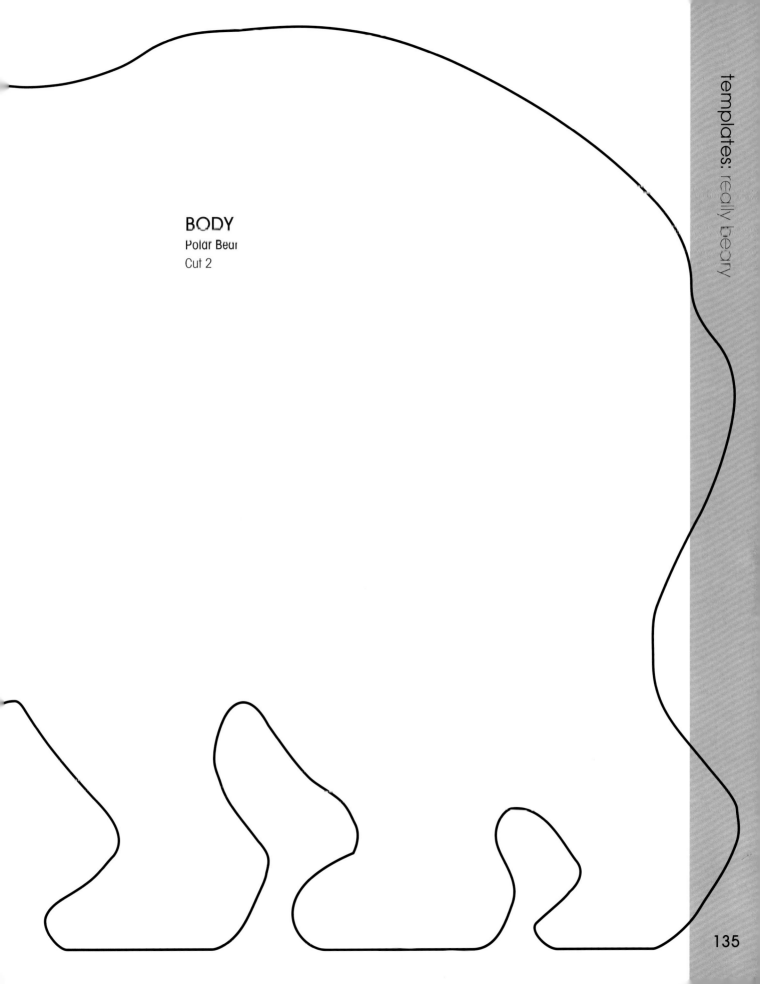

BODY
Polar Bear
Cut 2

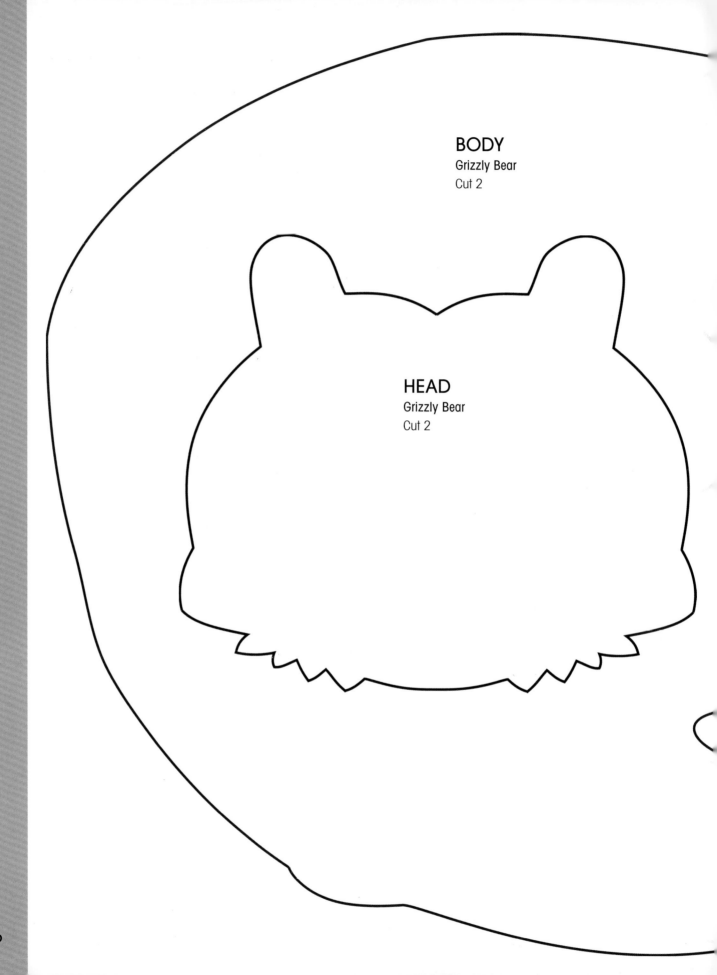

BODY
Grizzly Bear
Cut 2

HEAD
Grizzly Bear
Cut 2

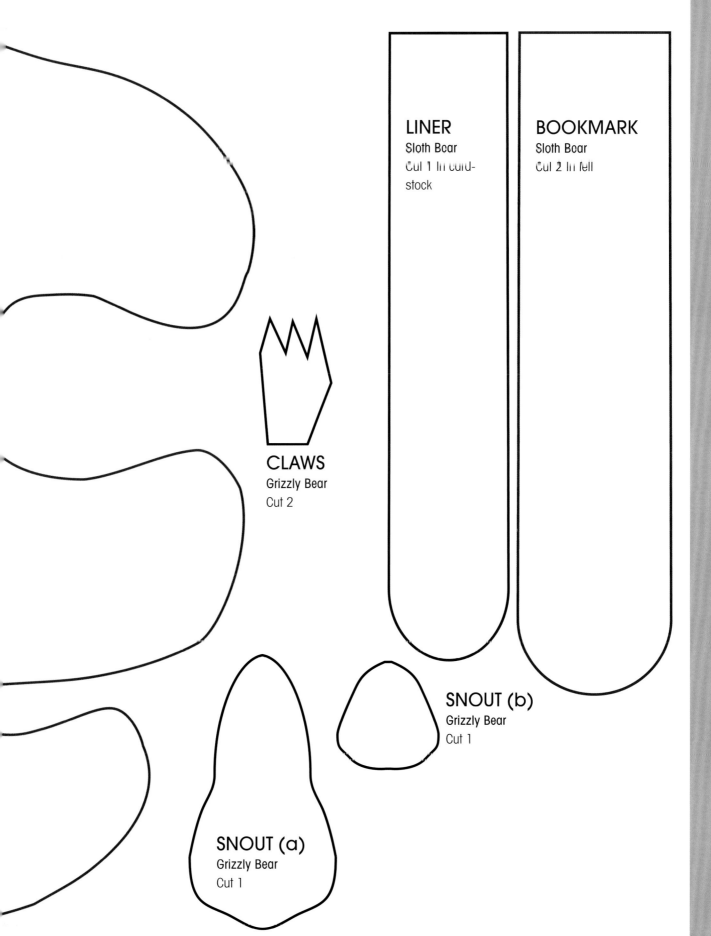

LINER
Sloth Bear
Cut 1 in card-stock

BOOKMARK
Sloth Bear
Cut 2 in felt

CLAWS
Grizzly Bear
Cut 2

SNOUT (b)
Grizzly Bear
Cut 1

SNOUT (a)
Grizzly Bear
Cut 1

137

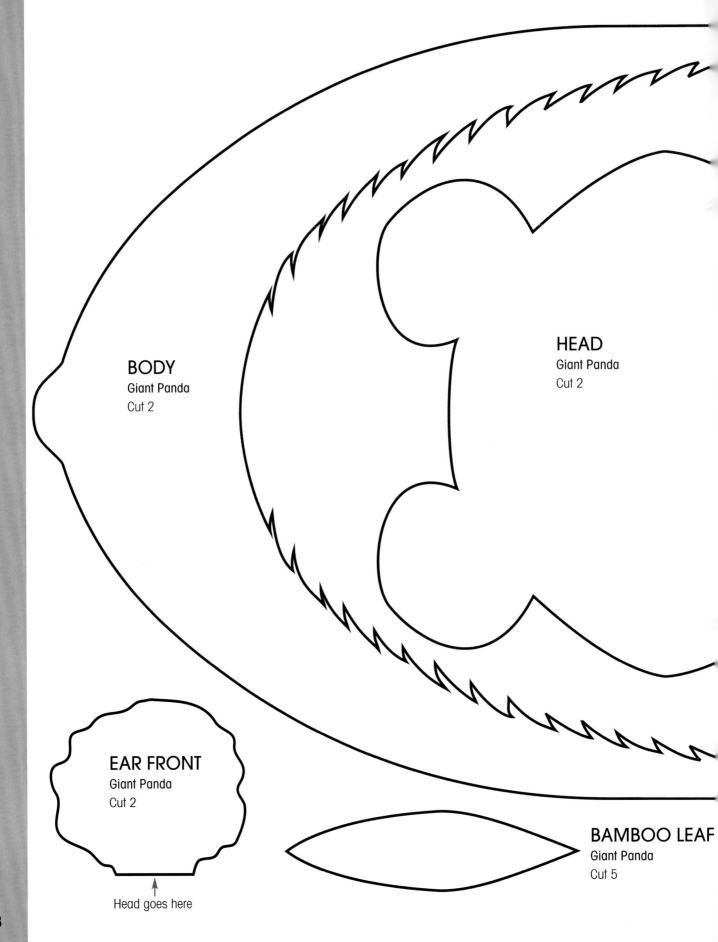

BODY
Giant Panda
Cut 2

HEAD
Giant Panda
Cut 2

EAR FRONT
Giant Panda
Cut 2

Head goes here

BAMBOO LEAF
Giant Panda
Cut 5

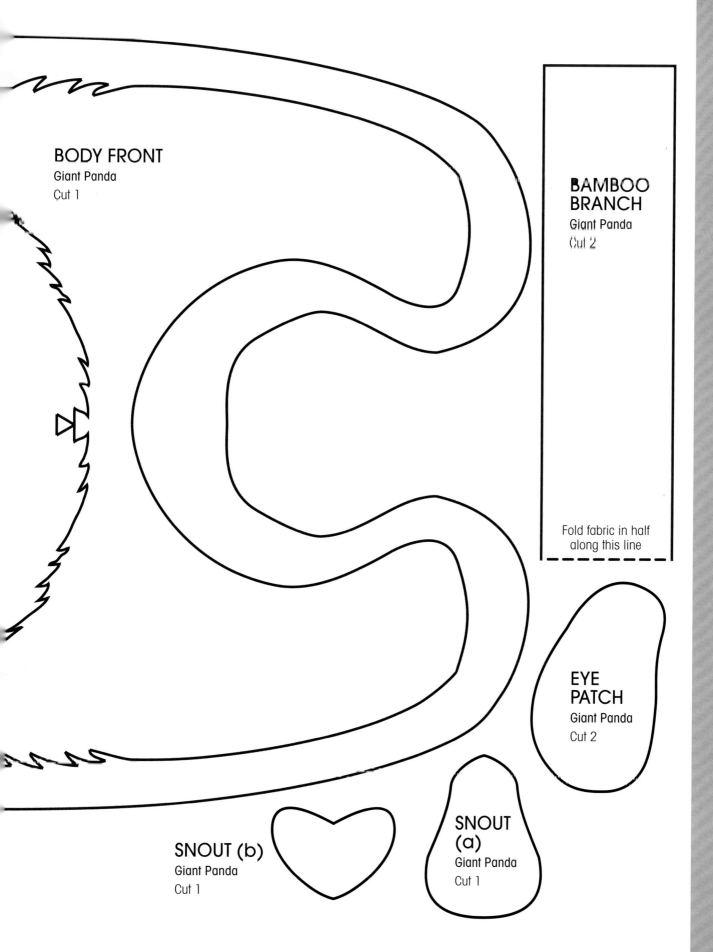

BODY FRONT
Giant Panda
Cut 1

BAMBOO BRANCH
Giant Panda
Cut 2

Fold fabric in half
along this line

EYE PATCH
Giant Panda
Cut 2

SNOUT (b)
Giant Panda
Cut 1

SNOUT (a)
Giant Panda
Cut 1

plush pretenders templates

This section includes the templates for all the bear figures in the Plush Pretenders chapter on pages 34-65 and the Autobearography bear found in the Fuzzy Crafts chapter on pages 72-79.

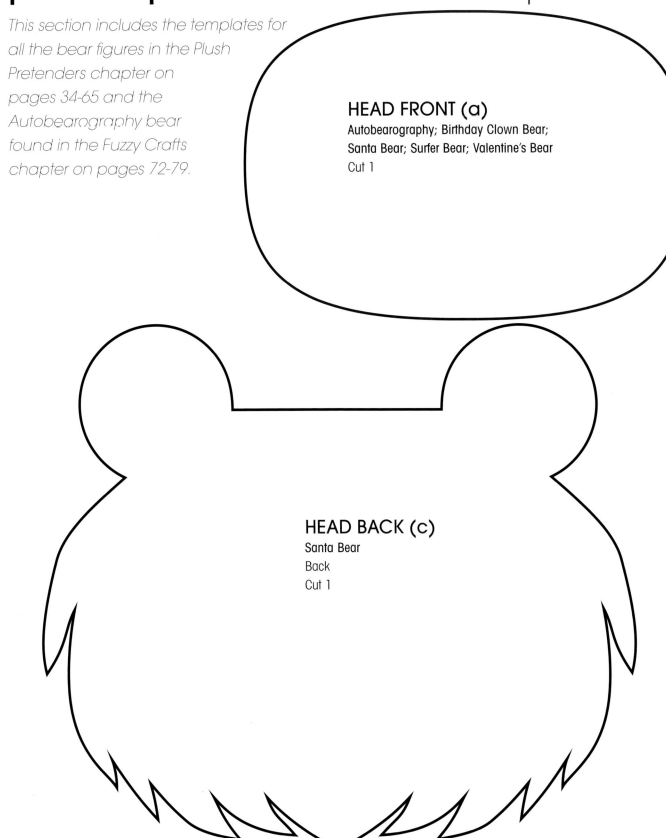

HEAD FRONT (a)
Autobearography; Birthday Clown Bear;
Santa Bear; Surfer Bear; Valentine's Bear
Cut 1

HEAD BACK (c)
Santa Bear
Back
Cut 1

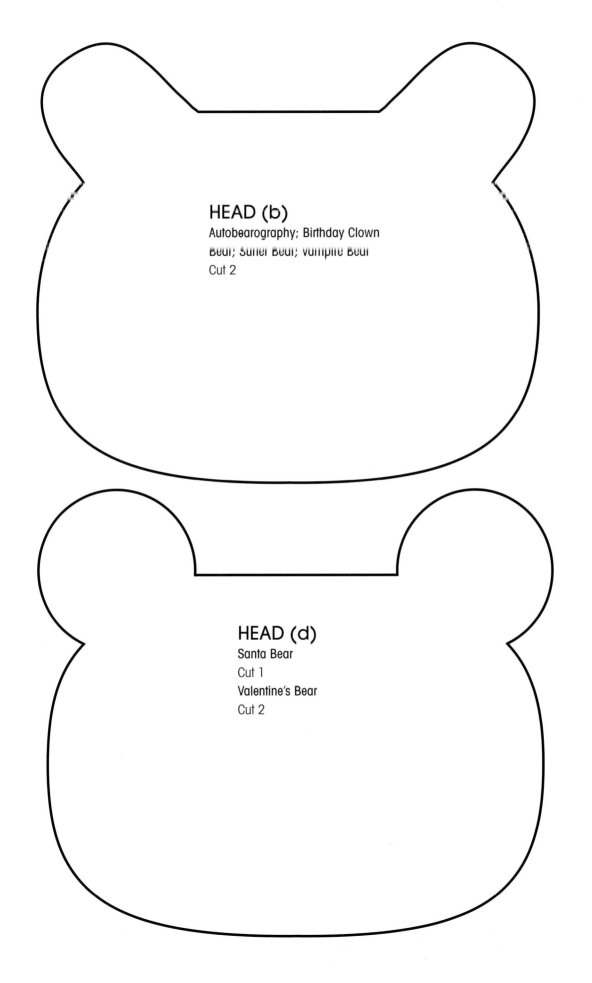

HEAD (b)

Autobearography; Birthday Clown
Bear; Surfer Bear; Vampire Bear
Cut 2

HEAD (d)

Santa Bear
Cut 1
Valentine's Bear
Cut 2

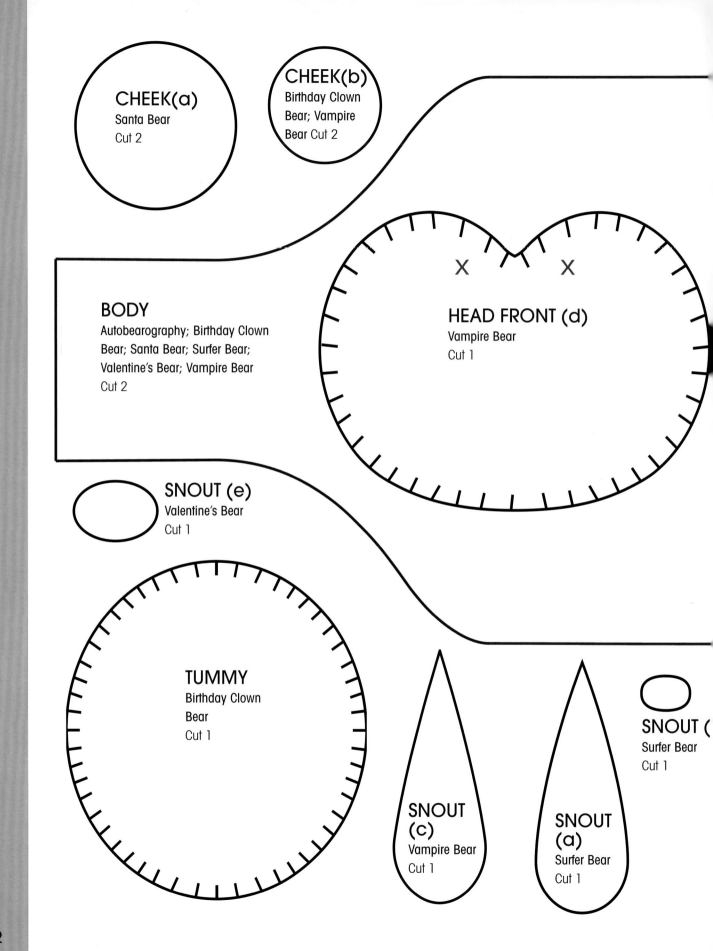

CHEEK(a)
Santa Bear
Cut 2

CHEEK(b)
Birthday Clown
Bear; Vampire
Bear Cut 2

BODY
Autobearography; Birthday Clown
Bear; Santa Bear; Surfer Bear;
Valentine's Bear; Vampire Bear
Cut 2

HEAD FRONT (d)
Vampire Bear
Cut 1

X   X

SNOUT (e)
Valentine's Bear
Cut 1

TUMMY
Birthday Clown
Bear
Cut 1

SNOUT (
Surfer Bear
Cut 1

SNOUT
(c)
Vampire Bear
Cut 1

SNOUT
(a)
Surfer Bear
Cut 1

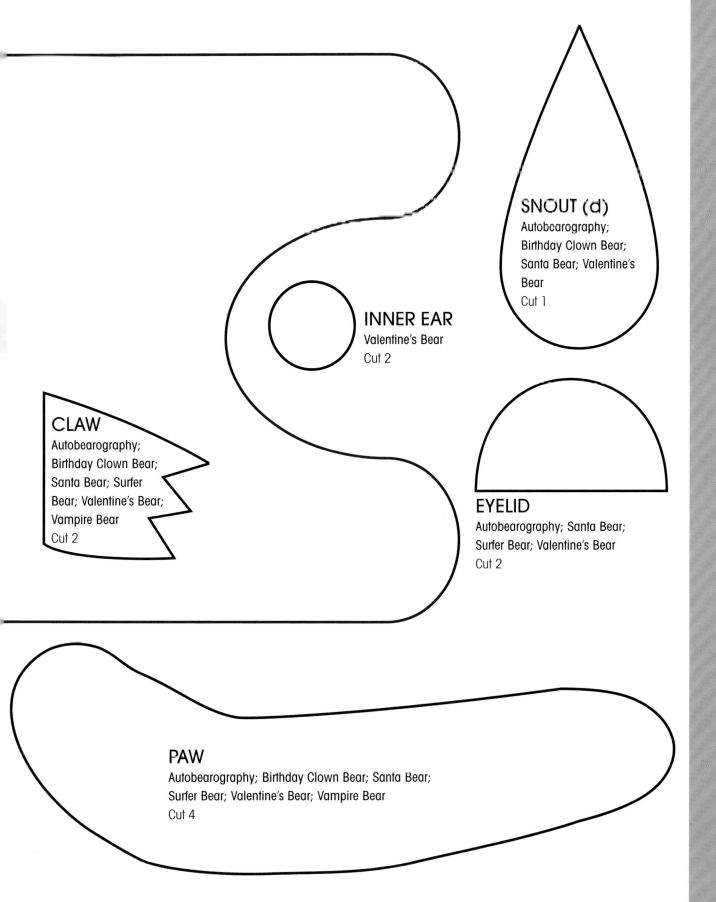

SNOUT (d)
Autobearography;
Birthday Clown Bear;
Santa Bear; Valentine's
Bear
Cut 1

INNER EAR
Valentine's Bear
Cut 2

EYELID
Autobearography; Santa Bear;
Surfer Bear; Valentine's Bear
Cut 2

CLAW
Autobearography;
Birthday Clown Bear;
Santa Bear; Surfer
Bear; Valentine's Bear;
Vampire Bear
Cut 2

PAW
Autobearography; Birthday Clown Bear; Santa Bear;
Surfer Bear; Valentine's Bear; Vampire Bear
Cut 4

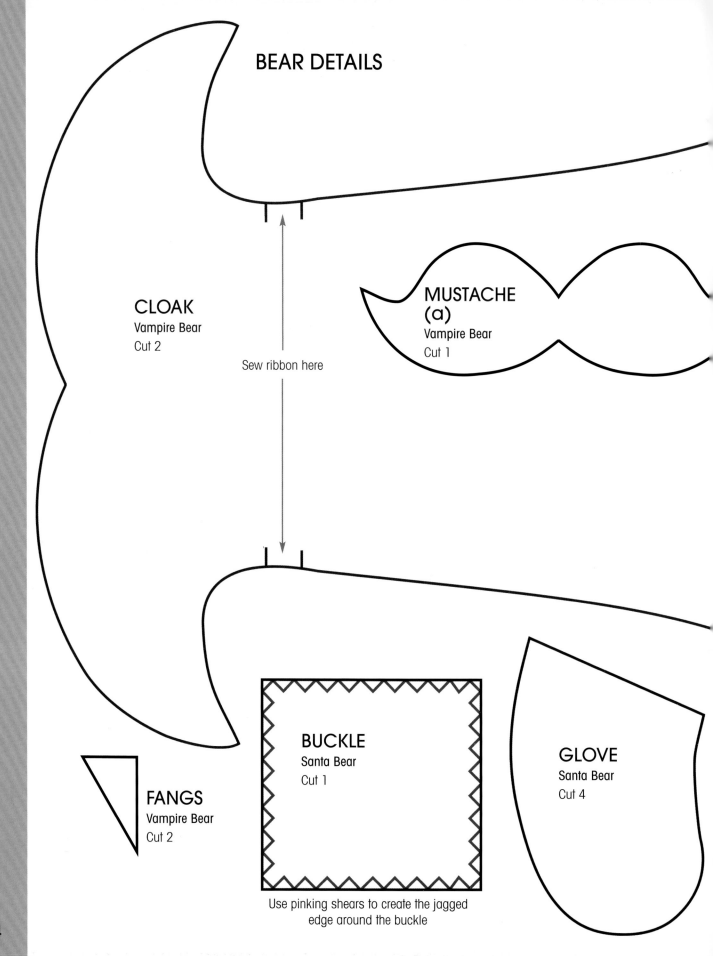

BEAR DETAILS

CLOAK
Vampire Bear
Cut 2

Sew ribbon here

MUSTACHE
(a)
Vampire Bear
Cut 1

FANGS
Vampire Bear
Cut 2

BUCKLE
Santa Bear
Cut 1

GLOVE
Santa Bear
Cut 4

Use pinking shears to create the jagged
edge around the buckle

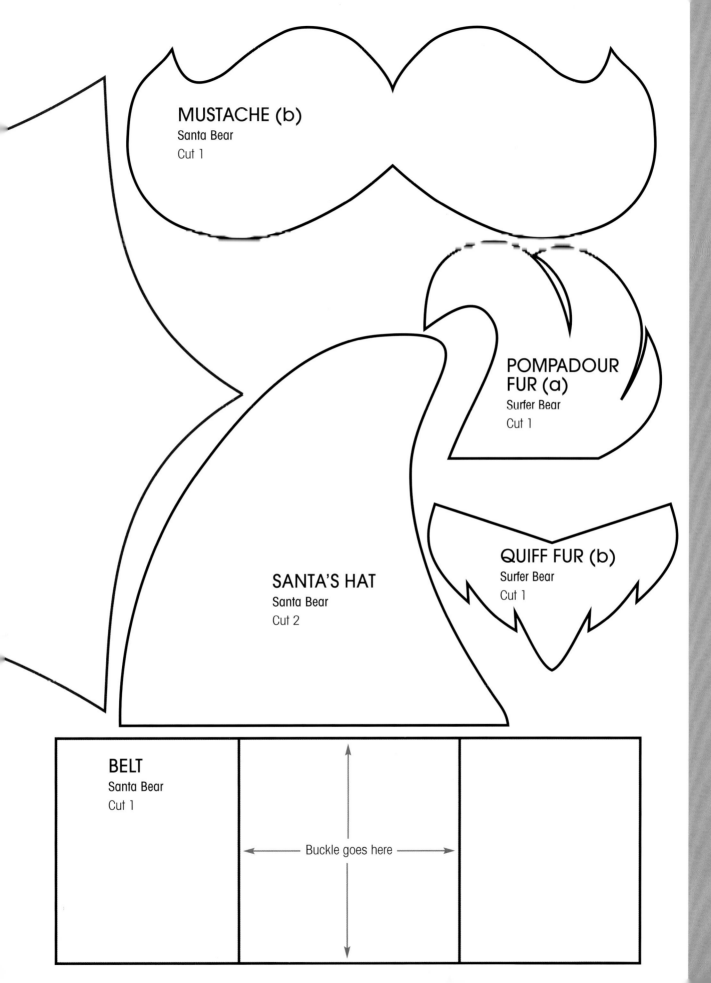

MUSTACHE (b)
Santa Bear
Cut 1

POMPADOUR
FUR (a)
Surfer Bear
Cut 1

QUIFF FUR (b)
Surfer Bear
Cut 1

SANTA'S HAT
Santa Bear
Cut 2

BELT
Santa Bear
Cut 1

Buckle goes here

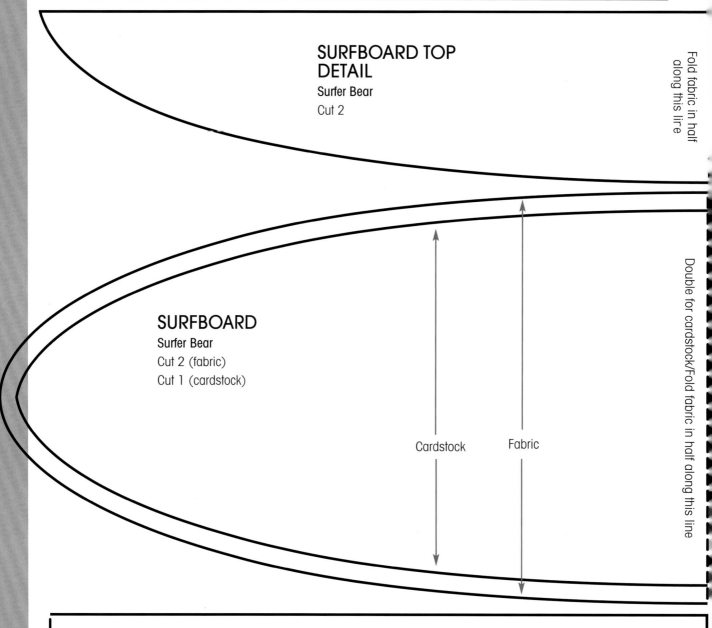

BELT Surfer Bear
Cut 1

X

SURFBOARD TOP DETAIL
Surfer Bear
Cut 2

Fold fabric in half along this line

SURFBOARD
Surfer Bear
Cut 2 (fabric)
Cut 1 (cardstock)

Cardstock   Fabric

Double for cardstock/Fold fabric in half along this line

Fold fabric here twice so that strip measures 6 x 75 cm

NECK RUFFLE
Birthday Clown Bear
Cut 3

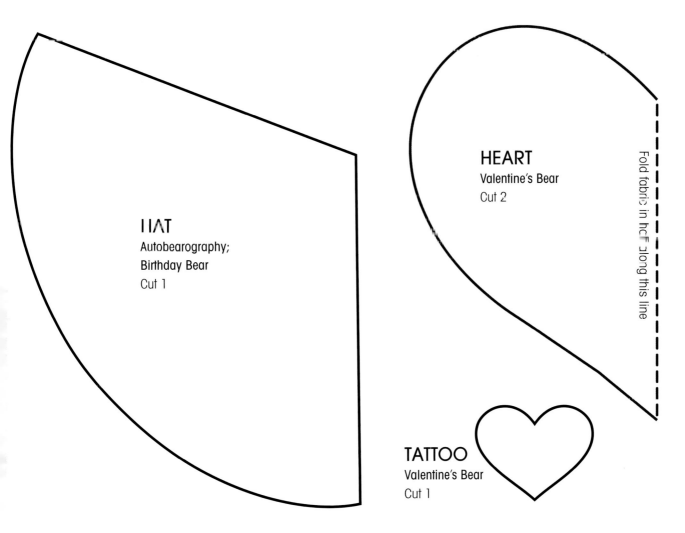

HAT
Autobearography;
Birthday Bear
Cut 1

HEART
Valentine's Bear
Cut 2

Fold fabric in half along this line

TATTOO
Valentine's Bear
Cut 1

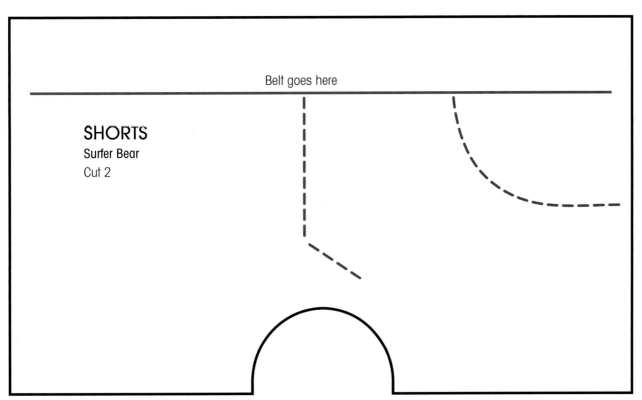

Belt goes here

SHORTS
Surfer Bear
Cut 2

other stuff templates

This final section includes all the templates for the rest of the projects in the book.

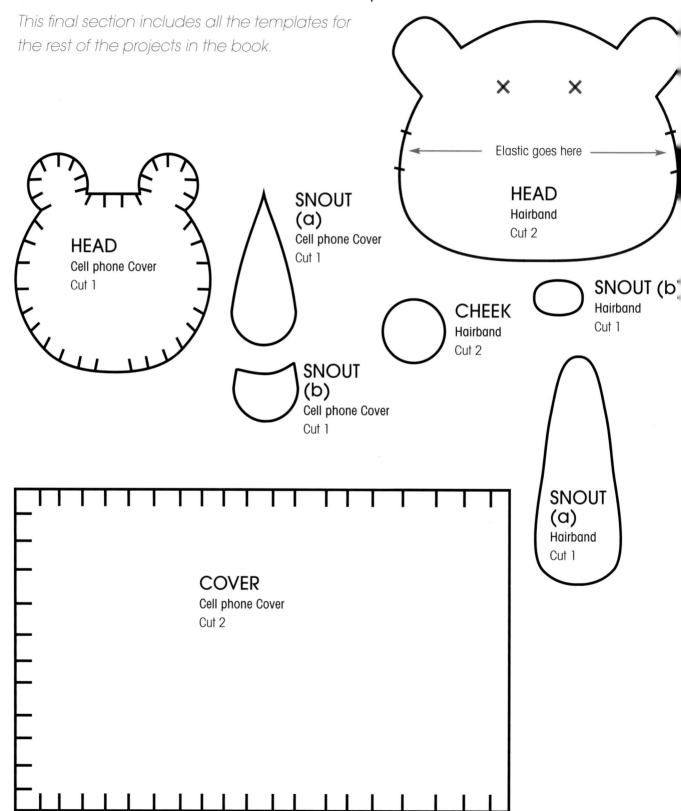

Elastic goes here

HEAD
Hairband
Cut 2

HEAD
Cell phone Cover
Cut 1

SNOUT (a)
Cell phone Cover
Cut 1

SNOUT (b)
Cell phone Cover
Cut 1

CHEEK
Hairband
Cut 2

SNOUT (b)
Hairband
Cut 1

SNOUT (a)
Hairband
Cut 1

COVER
Cell phone Cover
Cut 2

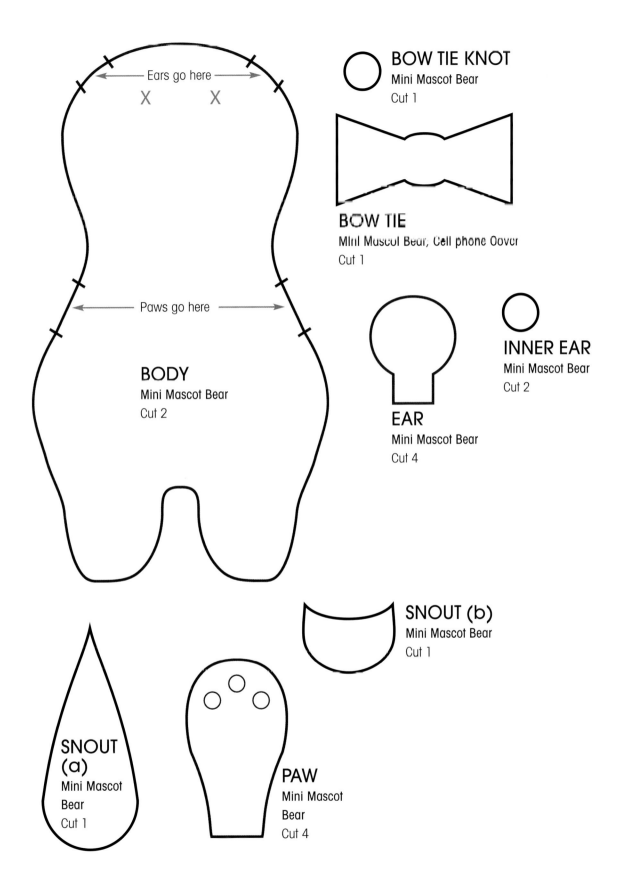

BOW TIE KNOT
Mini Mascot Bear
Cut 1

Ears go here
X   X

BOW TIE
Mini Mascot Bear, Cell phone Oover
Cut 1

INNER EAR
Mini Mascot Bear
Cut 2

Paws go here

BODY
Mini Mascot Bear
Cut 2

EAR
Mini Mascot Bear
Cut 4

SNOUT (b)
Mini Mascot Bear
Cut 1

SNOUT (a)
Mini Mascot Bear
Cut 1

PAW
Mini Mascot Bear
Cut 4

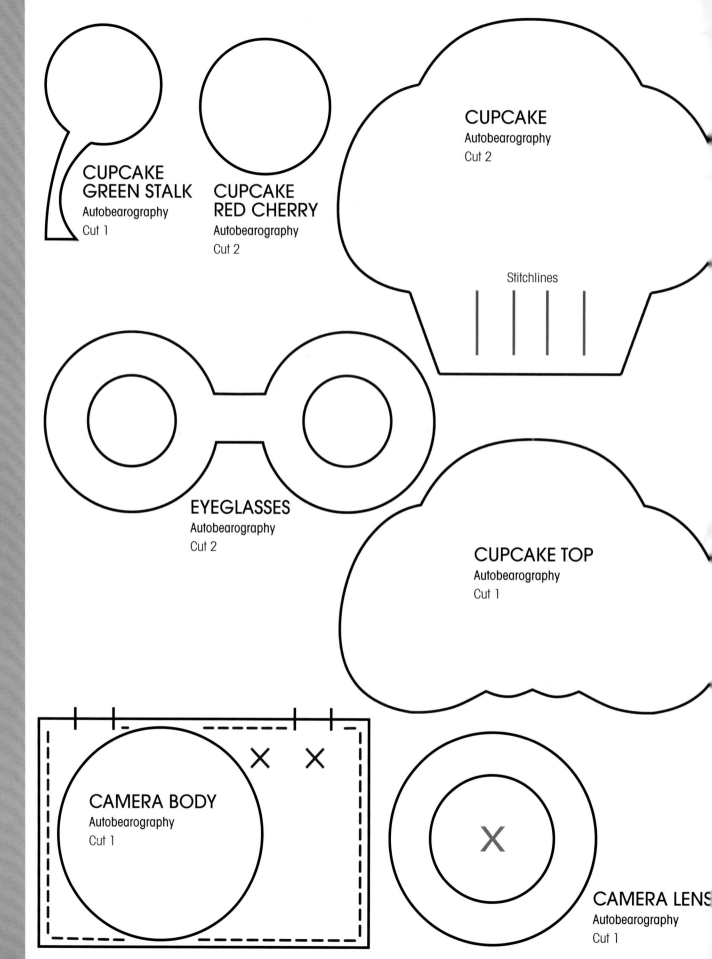

CUPCAKE GREEN STALK
Autobearography
Cut 1

CUPCAKE RED CHERRY
Autobearography
Cut 2

CUPCAKE
Autobearography
Cut 2

Stitchlines

EYEGLASSES
Autobearography
Cut 2

CUPCAKE TOP
Autobearography
Cut 1

CAMERA BODY
Autobearography
Cut 1

CAMERA LENS
Autobearography
Cut 1

Sew knitting here

Sew paws (a) here

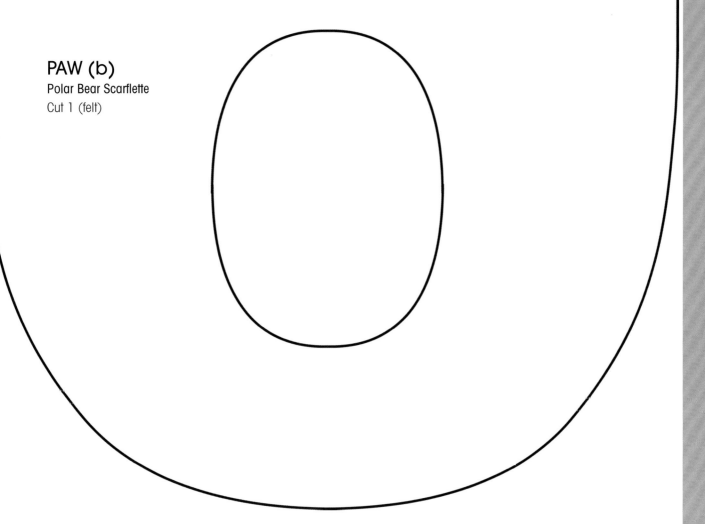

PAW (b)
Polar Bear Scarflette
Cut 1 (felt)

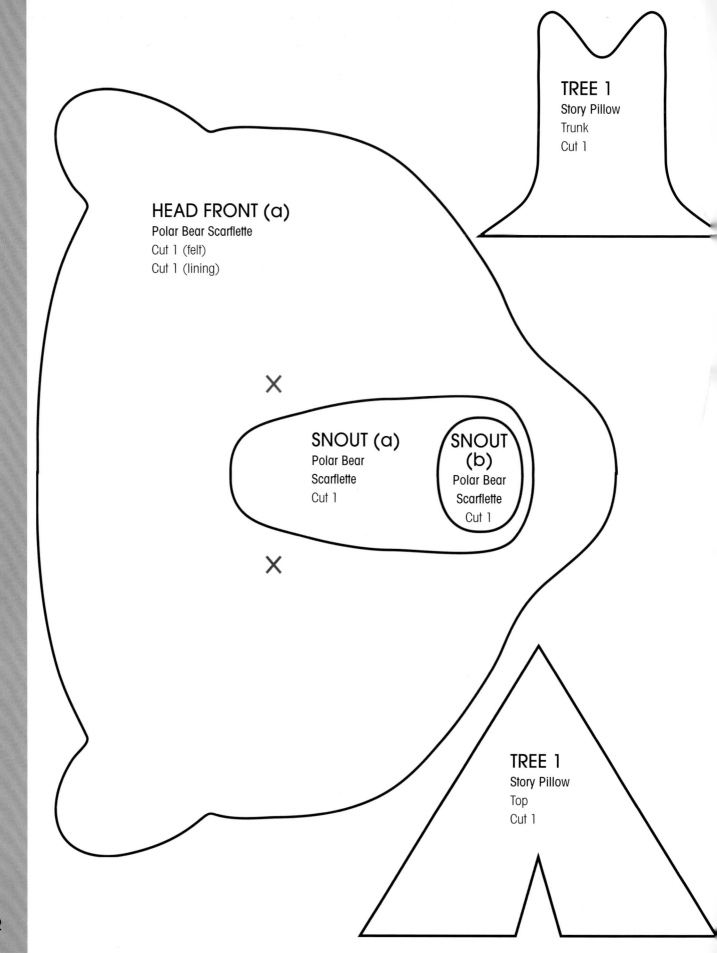

TREE 1
Story Pillow
Trunk
Cut 1

HEAD FRONT (a)
Polar Bear Scarflette
Cut 1 (felt)
Cut 1 (lining)

SNOUT (a)
Polar Bear
Scarflette
Cut 1

SNOUT
(b)
Polar Bear
Scarflette
Cut 1

TREE 1
Story Pillow
Top
Cut 1

Sew knitting here

HEAD BACK (B)
Polar Bear Scarflette
Cut 1 (felt)

SUN
MIDDLE
Cut 1

SUN
Story Pillow
Cut 1

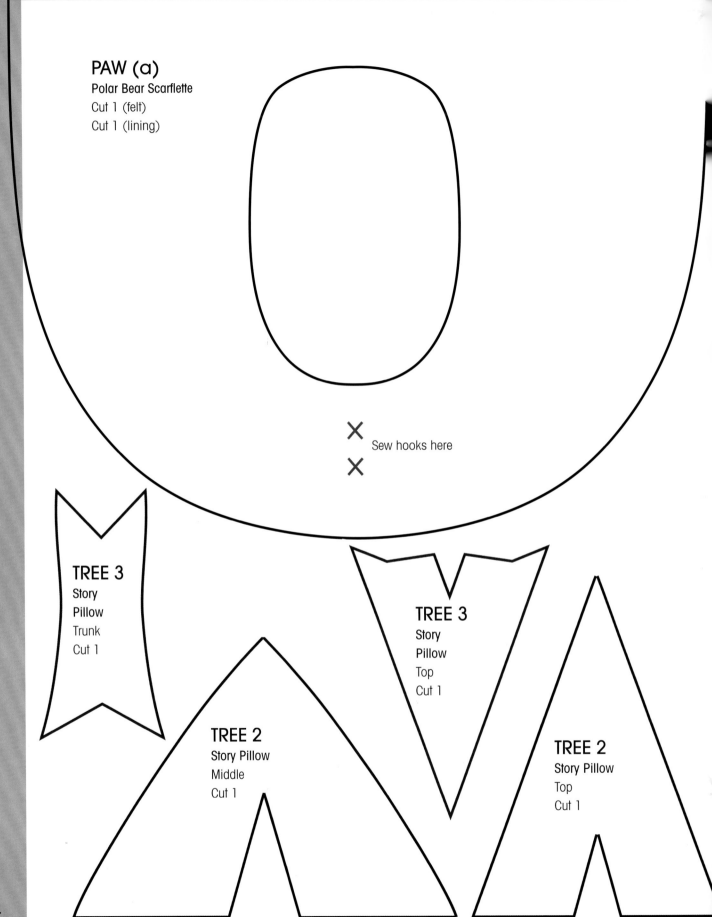

PAW (a)
Polar Bear Scarflette
Cut 1 (felt)
Cut 1 (lining)

Sew hooks here

TREE 3
Story
Pillow
Trunk
Cut 1

TREE 3
Story
Pillow
Top
Cut 1

TREE 2
Story Pillow
Middle
Cut 1

TREE 2
Story Pillow
Top
Cut 1

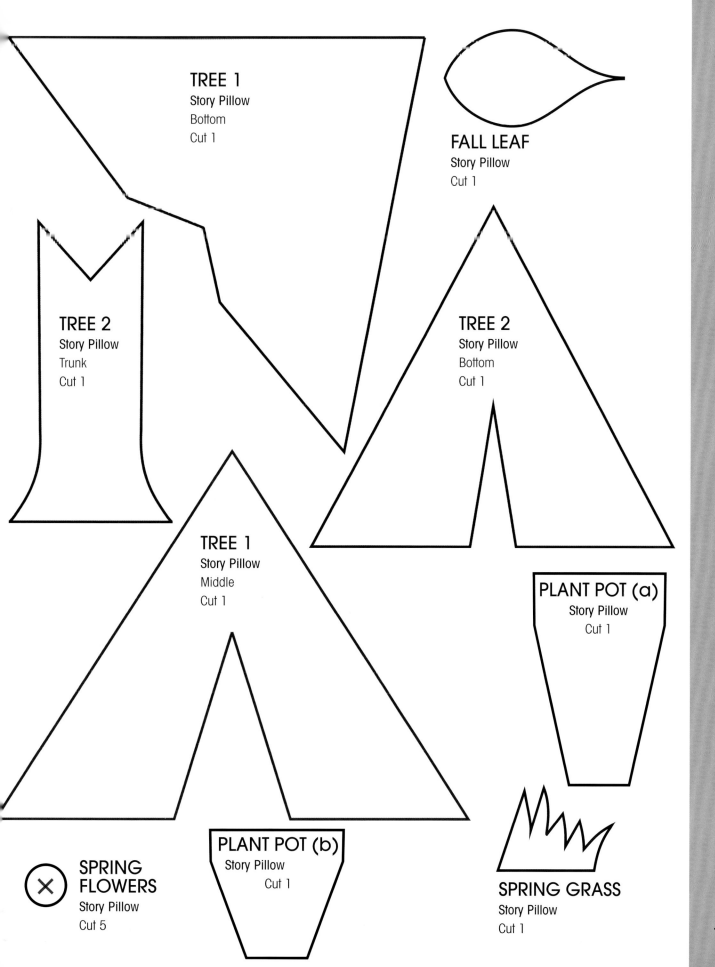

TREE 1
Story Pillow
Bottom
Cut 1

FALL LEAF
Story Pillow
Cut 1

TREE 2
Story Pillow
Trunk
Cut 1

TREE 2
Story Pillow
Bottom
Cut 1

TREE 1
Story Pillow
Middle
Cut 1

PLANT POT (a)
Story Pillow
Cut 1

SPRING FLOWERS
Story Pillow
Cut 5

PLANT POT (b)
Story Pillow
Cut 1

SPRING GRASS
Story Pillow
Cut 1

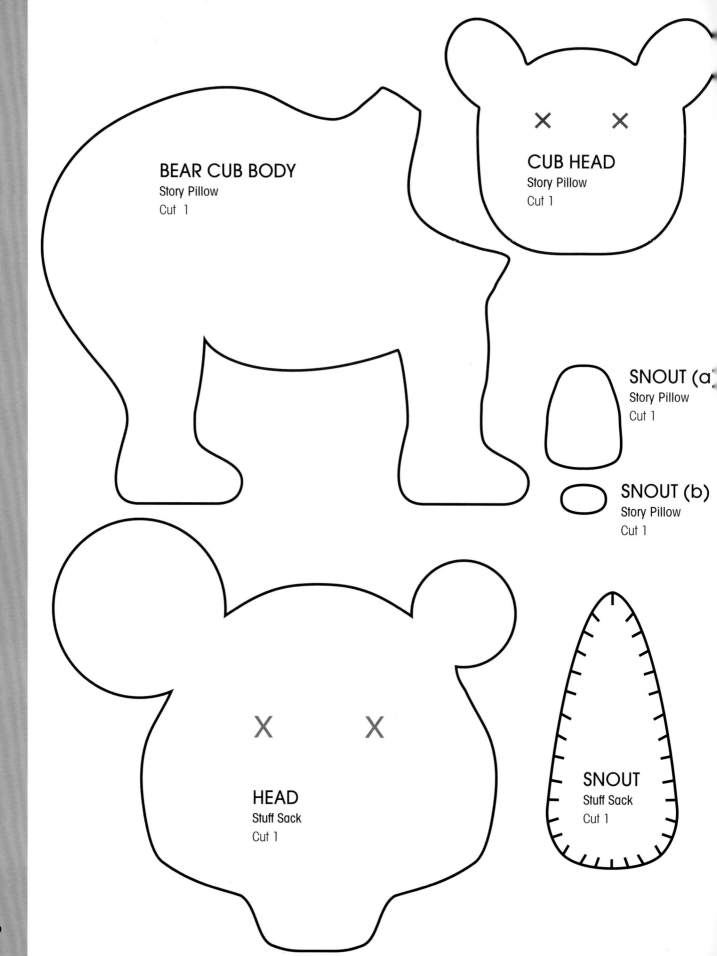

BEAR CUB BODY
Story Pillow
Cut 1

CUB HEAD
Story Pillow
Cut 1

SNOUT (a)
Story Pillow
Cut 1

SNOUT (b)
Story Pillow
Cut 1

HEAD
Stuff Sack
Cut 1

SNOUT
Stuff Sack
Cut 1

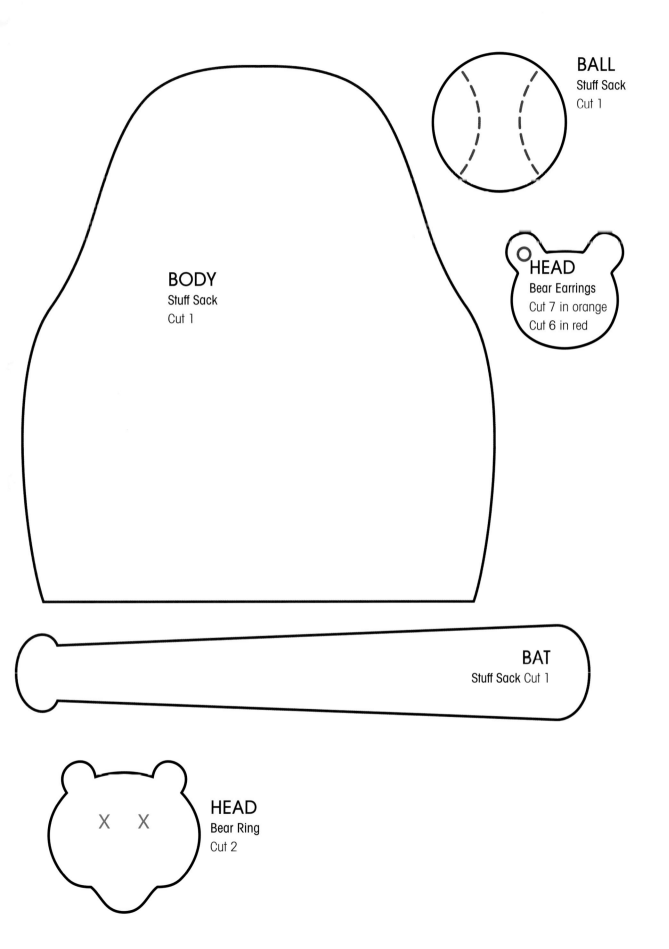

BALL
Stuff Sack
Cut 1

HEAD
Bear Earrings
Cut 7 in orange
Cut 6 in red

BODY
Stuff Sack
Cut 1

BAT
Stuff Sack Cut 1

X   X

HEAD
Bear Ring
Cut 2

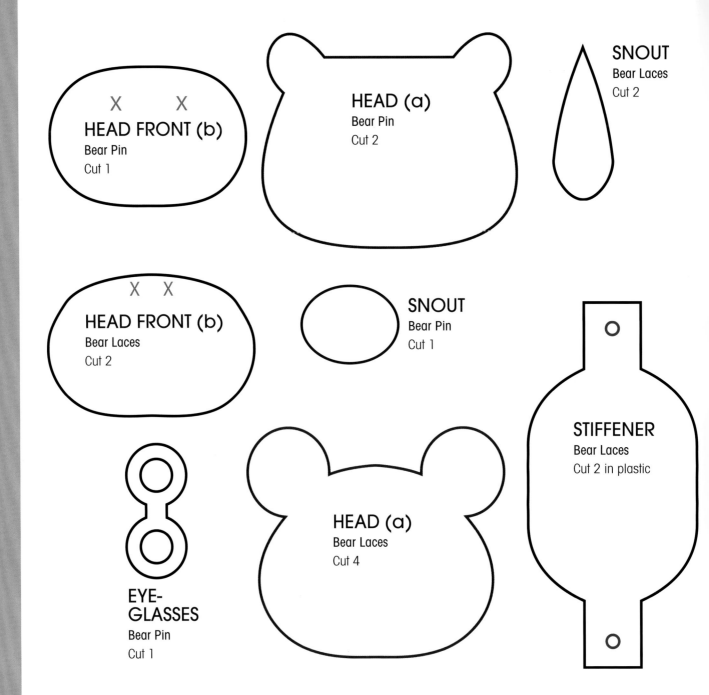

HEAD FRONT (b)
Bear Pin
Cut 1

HEAD (a)
Bear Pin
Cut 2

SNOUT
Bear Laces
Cut 2

HEAD FRONT (b)
Bear Laces
Cut 2

SNOUT
Bear Pin
Cut 1

STIFFENER
Bear Laces
Cut 2 in plastic

EYE-GLASSES
Bear Pin
Cut 1

HEAD (a)
Bear Laces
Cut 4

index

acknowledgments

Fil Rouge Press would like to thank Benjamin Rowling, Michael Craven, Janis Utton, Jenny Latham, Lily More, and Rosy Ngo for all their hard work on the book.